ACKNOWLEDGMENTS

Virginia Fugate, my loving and faithful partner, who typed every page of this manuscript through physical pain.

Carl Denti, my pastor, who inspired this work.

My Parents, who have always supported and encouraged me in my ministry.

Dr. Guyla Nelson, who edited my mistakes, leaving only a few for my humility.

Mary Updike, who funded this book's writing by faith. May she be made *ruler over many things and enter into the joy of the Lord* (Matthew 25:23).

Princess, my possessive cat who allowed me to use my desk for writing as long as she could lay on it next to me.

*Figurine artwork —
"Palm of My Hand"
was used on the cover
by permission of:
Roman, Inc. © 1986
555 Lawrence Ave.
Roselle, Illinois
60172-1599*

DEDICATION

to the glory of God

The author takes no personal credit for the information presented in this book. May God alone be glorified through this presentation of His Word.

> Psalm 115:1 – *Not unto us, Lord, not unto us, but unto thy name give glory, for thy mercy, and for thy truth's sake.*

What the Bible Says About...™
SUFFERING

Biblical Answers for Today's Pain and Suffering

by

J. Richard Fugate

A Bible Study for Pastors, Counselors, Teachers, and Serious Students

Published by
Foundation for Biblical Research™
Tempe, Arizona

All Scripture quotations are taken from the
Authorized King James Version,
New Scofield Reference Bible

What the Bible Says About . . . ™ *Suffering*
Biblical Answers for Today's Pain and Suffering

Copyright 1999 by
Foundation for Biblical Research ™
2401 W. Southern Ave., #219
Tempe, Arizona

Web site: www.rfugate.com
e-mail: cbg@rfugate.com

All rights reserved. No part of this publication may be reproduced, stored in an electronic system, or transmitted in any form or by any means, electronic, mechanical, photocopy, recording, or otherwise, without the prior permission of the copyright owner. Brief quotations may be used in literary review without permission.

Printed in the United States of America
ISBN   1-889700-35-5
Library of Congress
Catalog Card number
99-64664

WHAT THE BIBLE SAYS ABOUT...™

is a series designed to present the systematic development of the Bible as it speaks on specific subjects. All study is performed under the principle of 2 Timothy 2:15 – *Study to show thyself approved unto God, a workman that needeth not to be ashamed, rightly dividing the word of truth.* Selected passages have been studied in depth within their context from the original languages of Scripture. Word studies have been performed on each word that is translated in the semantic domain of suffering/pain. Much of the research used in the writing of this book was performed by the Foundation for Biblical Research.™ FBR is a nonprofit (not tax exempt) corporation that is dedicated to the discovery of the specific meaning of Scripture and the fully substantiated presentation of that meaning.

The opinions, illustrations, and applications given in this book represent years of practical experience in, and observation of, human suffering as well as the result of many personal hours of Biblical study. The author accepts full responsibility for these opinions, illustrations, and applications. To God alone be the glory for the Biblical information revealed herein.

Foundation for Biblical Research ™

Other books in this series are:

> *What the Bible Says About...*™
> ***Child Training***, ISBN 1-888306-51-3

TABLE OF CONTENTS

Introduction 1

SECTION ONE: SUFFERING IS COMMON TO MAN

Chapter

1. Why Mankind Suffers 9
2. How Mankind Suffers 19
3. Why Does God Allow Suffering? 33
4. How Man Faces Suffering 45
5. Fear of Death and Dying 53

SECTION TWO: ARE CHRISTIANS DIFFERENT?

6. Christians Are People, Too! 65
7. Christians Are Special People 75
8. All God's Children Need Training 81
9. Believer Training 101 – Who Is God? 93
10. Believer Training 201 – Trusting in God 101

Chapter

11. Believer Training 301 – Knowing God 109

12. Divine Discipline 119

SECTION THREE:
SUFFERING – THE CHRISTIAN'S BADGE

13. Christ and The Church 131

14. Christ's Sufferings Are Our Example 139

15. The Christian Walk 147

16. The Christian Soldier 157

17. The Benefits of Suffering 175

APPENDICES

A. The Bible as a Source of Information for Man .. 187

B. Israel and the Law/The Church
   and the new Covenant 197

C. Greek Words Relating to Suffering 213

Bibliography 219

INTRODUCTION

Are you suffering right now? Every member of the human race experiences suffering at one time or another in his or her life. Most people either think that suffering is somehow their fault, or that it is totally undeserved and therefore unfair. The basic question is this: Why suffering? From the beginning man has wondered how a loving God could allow His creation to suffer. The answers to these and many other questions will be set forth in this book.

What the Bible Says About . . . ™ *Suffering* is a logical presentation of the subject which allows an individual to understand why, how, and even the benefits of suffering. It is a systematic theology that can be utilized in place of psychological programs currently being used for counseling.

What the Bible Says About . . .™ *Suffering* is unique in that the subject is handled solely from the Biblical viewpoint. The author accepts the Bible as absolute truth and as infinitely superior to any human system of thinking. There has been no attempt to modify God's Word to make it compatible with human philosophies, psychology, sociology, religious views, or public opinion. God's Word is accepted as is, without human adulteration. The Bible is also accepted as living and powerful information that is as relevant today as in the day when it was first revealed. The reason the author absolutely accepts the Bible as the best source of information for man is explained in Appendix A. Every reader should study the explanation of this premise before beginning this book.

What This Book Is Not

What the Bible Says About . . .™ *Suffering* is not a pill that attempts to take away the pain of suffering. Pain is a grace gift from God that is meant to protect us from even worse suffering. Some children are born without sensors for pain in their nerve endings. Their parents have to watch them constantly to keep them from putting a finger (or a whole hand) into a fan blade, or from teasing a dog to bite them, or from cutting their skin with a knife or scissors. Pain is not something to be feared or eliminated in the normal course of life; it is something to be felt and understood.

This book is not meant to give solace, comfort, or empathy to the one who is presently suffering. There are excellent books already written along those lines: *Joni*, by Joni Eareckson Tada and *A Path Through Suffering*, by Elisabeth Elliot are two of the best. If you are in the midst of suffering and need to experience some hope immediately, we suggest that you read one of these. By contrast, *What the Bible Says About . . .*™ *Suffering* was written to prepare its readers to understand and conquer suffering and to learn how to counsel others who are not prepared. To illustrate the difference in the two types of book, let us say you find yourself stranded on a desert island in the Pacific Ocean. After walking for days and not seeing or hearing any hope of rescue, you come across a mini sub that has been beached on the island. It is in perfect shape, so that all you have to do is figure out how to operate it and you can escape. In carefully searching the sub, you find only one manual. It is a great volume of stories about other people and how they felt to be in your position. It gives detailed descriptions about how excited those people were to find the sub and how some even gave praise to God. Moving stories describe how long the journey was and how great it felt to reach home. However, this type of book does not tell you where the "on" switch is located on the sub, or how to navigate it, or how to read the maps.

What the Bible Says About . . . ™ *Suffering* is a technical book that provides only Biblical information. Of course, there will be some true stories given throughout this book in order to illustrate Biblical principles – some from the personal sufferings of the author's family; others from the recorded suffering of well-known Christians. However, it is our intention to offer the reader a Biblical understanding of pain and suffering and to use stories only to illustrate. We suggest that you study the book with your Bible open and check out all verse references given by the author.

A Personal Testimony

Suffering! A single word that encompasses everything from a slight ache to excruciating pain; from hurt feelings to mental and emotional anguish. Often we try to express our suffering with words such as "It hurts," or "It feels bad" – all of which seem completely inadequate to describe the depth of our pain and despair.

In our pain we seek help from others. We try family, friends, doctors, and/or counselors in our quest for relief. We try to explain how we feel with words, "The pain is here doctor," "I feel so bad," or "I'm so afraid." But more often than not, the help and understanding one receives from others falls short. In our continued search to receive understanding, we enhance our verbal expression of suffering with adjectives – more words such as:

excruciating, horrible, or it *really, really* hurts. But it seems the worse the pain is, the more lonely we feel in our suffering.

Lonely! Perhaps this word explains the torture that accompanies all types of suffering better than any other. Whether we keep our suffering to ourselves or whether we solicit sympathy from others, we always feel alone in our pain. The author's wife, Virginia Fugate, who has suffered with a chronic and increasingly painful condition for thirty years, stated:

> "There was a time when I responded to the question, 'How are you today?' with exactly how I was. At first people were truly concerned and wanted to help. Could they run an errand for me, could they bring a meal, have I tried the latest healing treatment (herbal, vitamin, touch therapy, acupuncture, or massage)? After trying their various treatments, and my condition worsened rather than improved, the looks on their faces revealed to me that they really didn't want to know the truth of how I was doing – not unless I could report improvement. Some began to treat me as if there must be a reason within me that caused me to be cursed – like some terrible unconfessed sin. Slowly, offers of help and concern began to fade away and friends and family went on with their lives. I don't blame them, after all who wants to hear bad news all the time? Who wants to feel helpless or face reminders that something like this could also happen to them?
>
> "After a while I tried to keep my suffering to myself. I would smile, thank them for asking, and do my best to avoid telling them that I wasn't fine. I felt so alone with the pain. I could be in a room full of

people – talking, laughing, loving, caring people – and still feel painfully alone. I became imprisoned in pain, isolated, alone no matter where I was. And, loneliness is the worst suffering of all!

"But then I discovered that I am never really alone because *God is our refuge and strength, a very present help in trouble* (Psalm 46:1). He has promised, *He healeth the broken in heart, and bindeth up their wounds* (Psalm 147:3). No longer must I suffer in lonely silence for I always have God as my refuge and my ever-present companion.

"Although I have received some comfort from reading other books about suffering, it has been the Biblical information contained in this book that has given me victory over suffering."

Virginia Fugate

SECTION ONE

SUFFERING IS COMMON TO MAN

Romans 5:17 *For if by one man's offense death reigned by one, much more they who receive abundance of grace and of the gift of righteousness shall reign in life by one, Jesus Christ.*

I Corinthians 15:22 *For as in Adam all die, even so in Christ shall all be made alive;*

Chapter 1

WHY MANKIND SUFFERS

Man did not always experience a life of suffering. Original creation was perfectly made for living in peace and harmony.

> Genesis 1:31 – *And God saw every thing that he had made, and, behold, it was very good. And the evening and the morning were the sixth day.*

There was no pain, no sickness, no depravation of any kind. Man did not even know about death, let alone experience a fear of dying. He was the center of creation and it all seemed to be made just for him.

The First of Mankind

God created a *perfect* environment for mankind to possess and enjoy. There were no dangers to harm him, including himself. Peace, prosperity, and fulfillment were his life (Genesis 1:28, 29; 2:5, 6, 10-16, 21-25).

- **He had a lifelong purpose for his existence** –to be fruitful, multiply, and fill the earth; to subdue (conquer) the earth; to have dominion (rulership) over fish, fowl, and every living thing that moves on the earth. No need to "find himself" or to do meaningless work.

- **He had abundant food provided without effort.** No sixteen-hour days fighting the ground, weeds, and hostile environment to eke out a mere existence. (For all but the past one hundred years, man has needed to work from sunup to sundown just to provide food and shelter.)

- **He had a mist that arose from the ground to water the garden perfectly.** No hurricanes, tornadoes, hail storms, or even rain to interfere or damage the crops.

- **He had pure water for drinking and bathing.** Eden was the origin of four rivers including the Euphrates. No pollution up stream to taint his supply.

- **He had some light duties of tilling and guarding the garden.** No bugs, no weeds, no soil too acid or too alkaline – just break up the ground and keep the giraffe from grazing too much.

- **He had plenty of pets.** Nobody ate anybody in Eden; even the serpent was not dangerous.

- **He enjoyed a marriage made literally in Heaven with a woman who was both his soul mate and physical mate.** No battle over leadership; the man (ISH) was to lead, and the woman (ISHA – out of man) was to support, encourage, and comfort in her role as a helper fit for him.

- **He had a totally peaceful environment.** No delinquent kids, no in-laws, no neighbors, no crime, no wars, no sickness or injury, no dying, no sin, no lust to sin. No wonder Eden is sometimes called paradise.

- **He had volition – the right and the responsibility to make his own choices.** Not free will to make choices outside of the Plan or Will of God, but to make choices subject to bonafide tests with accountability.

- **He had a close and personal fellowship with his Creator.** Not the separation and searching man has experienced since Eden.

But, it was not God's Plan to leave man in paradise to live an idyllic life devoid of all suffering without demonstrating his willingness to submit to the Creator/God.

Man was designed to worship his Creator God – to consider himself as a subordinate in creation, not as an equal. Throughout history man has repeatedly seen himself as the center of all things and to think everything revolves around himself.

The Test

God set up a test for man in the Garden either to accept God's right to rule over him or instead to choose to assert his own, independent, self-rule. He has set forth this challenge to man throughout human history. Not only here in the Garden, but to Abraham, to Jacob, to the Nation of Israel, and to countless others God has said, "Will you hear and obey – deny yourself and follow me?"

> Genesis 2:16, 17 – *And the Lord God commanded the man, saying, Of every tree of the garden thou mayest freely eat; But of the tree of the knowledge of good and evil, thou shalt not eat of it; for in the day that thou eatest thereof thou shalt surely die.*

We have no revelation as to how long Adam and Eve obeyed God and avoided that deadly tree. What we do know is that, unlike men and women today, Adam and Eve had no internal lusts to tempt them to disobey God. They were truly innocent in deed and thought. Therefore, God allowed them to be tempted from outside of themselves by the fallen angel, Satan, through the most subtle (crafty) beast in creation, the serpent.

> Genesis 3:1 – *Now the serpent was more subtle than any beast of the field which the Lord God had made. And he said unto the woman, Yea, hath God said, Ye shall not eat of every tree of the garden?*

Eve was completely deceived by Satan's lies, the beauty of the fruit, and the possibility of becoming as wise as God (Genesis 3:2-6). So, she ate. Adam, knowing fully well that he was choosing to defy God, also did eat. Thereby, sin entered into the human race:

> Romans 5:12 – *Wherefore, as by one man sin entered into the world, and death by sin, and so death passed upon all men, for all have sinned.*

NOTE: One might argue that it is unfair for God to judge the entire human race for the actions of one man. However, there is no reason, except for the most arrogant of men or women, to think we would not have failed the test if given the chance. Not only that, *all have sinned, and come short of the glory of God* (Romans 3:23).

There has never been, or ever will be, a member of the human race (except Jesus Christ) who submitted his will to God, who has never sinned, who has measured up to the perfectly righteous standard of God. *There is none righteous, no, not one* (Romans 3:10).

The Fall's Effect on Mankind

Dead, dying, and damned. This is man's condition after Adam's willful transgression. These three terms refer to man's spirit, body, and soul. God told Adam *for in the day that thou eatest thereof thou shalt surely die* (Genesis 2:17b). The word translated *"surely die"* from the Hebrew is intensive and means a violent death, or a process of physically dying, or even multiple deaths. Let's see how man's essence was affected by the Fall.

Spirit–Dead. At the moment Adam sinned, he died spiritually, and death always entails a separation. His relationship with God was severed, his world came under the rulership of Satan's world system, and his thinking became controlled by the lusts of his flesh. This is the condition God finds man in today – spiritually dead and separated:

> Ephesians 2:1-3 – *And you hath he made alive, who were dead in trespasses and sins*;

> John 3:5b – *Except a man be born of water and of the Spirit, he cannot enter into the kingdom of God.*

Body–Dying. Adam's sin resulted in mankind's becoming mortal, subject to physical death. In other words, Adam began the aging process. There is no telling how long physical life would have lasted in the Garden, with an organically pure diet and clean water, and without catastrophes or illnesses.

(We do know that before the Flood humans lived to be about 900 years old – Genesis 5:5-31.)

> Romans 5:14a – *Nevertheless, death reigned from Adam to Moses, even over them that had not sinned after the similitude of Adam's transgression,*
>
> I Corinthians 15:22a – *For as in Adam all die,*
>
> Hebrews 9:27a – *And as it is appointed unto men once to die,*

Soul–Damned. The soul is the animation of the body and lives as long as the brain functions. It is generally thought to consist of a person's mentality, emotion, conscience, and will. When the brain dies, the soul is released and sent to Hades (unless saved) and then resurrected for the Final Judgment. After this it is cast into the *literal* lake of fire.

> Hebrews 9:27 – *And as it is appointed unto men once to die, but after this the judgment.*
>
> Revelation 20:14, 15 – *And death and hades were cast into the lake of fire. This is the second death. And whosoever was not found written in the book of life was cast into the lake of fire.*

As if being dead, dying, and damned were not bad enough, Adam developed, and we each inherit, a sinful nature which constantly tempts us to do evil and to disobey God. This nature is Scripturally defined as the sin nature (the sin, the flesh, the old man). It corrupts our will, our thinking, our conscience, and our emotions.

> Romans 8:7, 8 – *Because the carnal mind is enmity against God; for it is not subject to the law of God, neither, indeed, can be. So, then, they that are in the flesh[1] cannot please God.*

> Galatians 5:19, 20a – *Now the works of the flesh are manifest, which are these: adultery, fornication, uncleanness, lasciviousness, Idolatry, sorcery, hatred, strife, jealousy, wrath, factions, seditions, heresies, Envyings, murders, drunkenness, revelings, and the like;*

Every member of the human race born since Adam and Eve fell has entered the world as an enemy of God under the influence of his own sinful nature, and destined for the second death. It is no longer necessary for Satan to test man personally; each person is tested within himself and each one falls.

> Romans 3:10-12 – *As it is written, There is none righteous, no, not one: There is none that understandeth, there is none that seeketh after God. They are all gone out of the way, they are together become unprofitable; there is none that doeth good, no, not one.*

How can man overcome the cursing effects of sin? There are only two ways to approach the problem of man's lost and condemned condition:

- One solution which has been tried since Cain (Adam's first son) and throughout every generation by millions of poor, deceived souls is RELIGION. Man has futilely attempted to bridge the distance between his unrighteous, depraved condition and the absolute righteousness of God by offering up the tainted sacrifices of his own works. This is similar to the little boy who desperately wanted to be taller, pulling on his bootstraps in order to gain height. The little boy will not grow taller by his own efforts and neither will man gain the approval of God by his own efforts – good works.

Isaiah 64:6 – *But we are all as an unclean thing, and all our righteousnesses are as filthy rags*;

Romans 3:23 – *For all have sinned, and come short of the glory of God.*

- The only real solution is the personal acceptance (faith) of God's grace gift of salvation (deliverance from your present position in Adam, your personal sins, and from your future judgment).

John 3:16-18 – *For God so loved the world, that he gave his only begotten Son, that whosoever believeth in him should not perish, but have everlasting life. For God sent not his Son into the world to condemn the world, but that the world through him*

> might be saved. He that believeth on him is not condemned; but he that believeth not is condemned already, because he hath not believed in the name of the only begotten Son of God.

Which solution have you chosen? The one where you proudly place your good deeds before God, who must reject them, or the one where you humbly accept Christ's sacrifice on the cross in your behalf?

> Titus 3:5a – *Not by works of righteousness which we have done, but according to his mercy he saved us,*

Even after trusting in Christ, the newly-born Christian still lives in this world and is subject to physical death and suffering. However, God has given Christians special power to overcome adversity and to glorify Him in the process.

Summary

Why does mankind suffer? We can see that one major reason is because of the Fall. When Adam failed the test of obedience (as any of us would have done), Paradise was indeed lost. We will see in the next chapter what this meant to our loss of ease and comfort. However, I pray that the reader will grasp the full significance of God's judgment on all mankind that was due to Adam's sin and the inheritance of *"sin with us,"* the sin nature. More importantly, that he has accepted God's only grace solution for his personal position in Adam – trusting in Christ. *Neither is there salvation in any other: for there is none other name under heaven given among men, whereby we must be saved* (Acts 4:12).

This is the testimony of one who accepted the Christ solution:

> John Newton's tombstone carries these words written by himself, *John Newton, clerk, once an infidel and Libertine, a servant of slavers in Africa, was, by the rich mercy of our Lord and Savior Jesus Christ, preserved, restored, pardoned, and appointed to preach the faith he had so long labored to destroy.* *
>
> John Newton wrote the hymn *Amazing Grace* from experience.

---

* *The One Year Book of Hymns*, 1995, Tyndale House Publishers, Wheaton, IL.

[1] Greek, *sarx*, "flesh." This word describes the physical, material flesh of man as in flesh and blood. However, it is also used to describe the material nature of man as compared to his soulish, non-material nature. Here, it refers to a man under the influence of his natural, material nature apart from any spiritual influence.

Romans 8:21, 22 *Because the creation itself also shall be delivered from the bondage of corruption into the glorious liberty of the children of God. For we know that the whole creation groaneth and travaileth in pain together until now.*

Chapter 2

How Mankind Suffers

The Corruption of Paradise

In the last chapter we saw that much of what man suffers today is a result of his failing the test to obey God while living in the perfect environment of Eden. In this chapter we will describe how Paradise changed after the Fall. We will also introduce man's greatest adversary – Satan.

The effects of the Fall on mankind and creation have continued throughout time and cause much of our suffering today.

- **No more perfect environment outside of the Garden.** Hostile weather conditions became a major factor of life. Hurricanes, tornadoes, earthquakes, floods, droughts, and subzero temperatures cause random suffering to the human race.

- **No more effortless food supply.** The ground was cursed with thorns and thistles, and became difficult to till. Poverty, starvation, and famine have caused millions of men, women, and children to suffer from this curse.

- **No easy childbearing.** Conception and child birth were cursed with much pain and suffering. Miscarriages, breach babies, stillborns, and other complications are some of the suffering that results from this curse.

- **No more would the woman be a natural helpmeet for the man.** She is now cursed with having a strong desire to control her husband, and yet he is designed to rule over her. The battle of the sexes begins. There is not a husband or wife who has not been affected by this curse.

- **No more friendly pets of the wild animals.** No longer vegetarians, some would eat man in a second. Stinging and biting insects, venomous reptiles, and other distortions of the animal world now plague.

- **No children would be conceived in innocence.** They will all be born with the sin nature passed through their parents. Of course, each child would also have a will of its own, desiring the same autonomy its parents expressed in their disobedience. Child rebellion from Cain forward brings suffering to parents. (See *What the Bible Says About...*™ ***Child Training***, 2nd Edition.)

How Mankind Suffers

- **No more innocence in conscience, thinking, feelings, or will.** The sin nature corrupts all of these areas of the soul with evil (that which is against the plan of God). From the sin nature originate adultery, fornication, idolatry, hatred, jealousy, selfish ambition, rebellion and all other lusts. Man suffers from these attitudes and also from the sinful acts they produce: brawling, plundering, war; scarred unmarrieds, ruined marriages, destroyed children; stealing, drug sales, extortion, bribery; even destruction of entire nations who abandon moral conduct.

- **No more running around the garden naked.** Our guilt and shame will avoid an open relationship with God and others. Our sin nature will distort anything good and innocent into something vile. This is the epitome of a bad self image – and it cannot be fixed by psycho-babble.

- **No more fellowship with God since the spirit is dead; but man can be "born again," or "born from above," through faith in Christ and this will end the suffering of separation from God.**

John 3:6, 7 – *That which is born of the flesh is flesh; and that which is born of the Spirit is spirit. Marvel not that I said unto thee, Ye must be born again.*

Ephesians 2:5 – *Even when we were dead in sins, hath made us alive together with Christ (by grace ye are saved),*

NOTE: References to a "Christian" or a "believer" throughout the remainder of this book refer to such a regenerated person.

- **No more an always-living soul destined to eternal life with God.** Man is now destined to suffer judgment and an eternal life of damnation **unless** he is saved by God (Hebrews 9:27; Revelation 20:6).

- **No more perfect physical health since the body is now degenerating (dying).** Man since the Garden will suffer disease, injury, sickness, plague, and death (Job 34:15; Psalm 144:4). The only way to overcome this suffering permanently is by the resurrection designed by God for "believers" (John 11:25; I Corinthians 15:42-45). Christians should not expect an earthly life free from physical suffering by any means.

We should, however, keep in mind that no matter how severely we suffer, God is always in control and can enable us to conquer or endure the suffering. *My grace is sufficient for thee; for my strength is made perfect in weakness* (II Corinthians 12:9b). Christians need not live a life of fear of Satan (Romans 8:38), or of physical death (Hebrews 2:15), or of bondage to their sin nature (Romans 8:15). Take courage! God has a means to conquer every worry, fear, doubt, or real-life calamity which we must face in this corrupted world.

> **NOTE:** One of the most debilitating false doctrines that has been taught in some Christian circles is that suffering comes only to those believers who are in sin or who lack faith in God and that God *always* heals those who have enough faith (like Elmer Gantry's portrayal). The false doctrine of temporal prosperity (family, financial, and health) clearly stems from not rightly dividing the Word of God. While Israel was administered by the Old

Covenant (The Law), it indeed experienced physical prosperity; however, this was true *only if they kept The Law* (Deuteronomy 28:1-13; Joshua 1:8; John 9:1-3). The New Covenant administered by the Holy Spirit is a spiritual covenant with the Church, guaranteeing all true believers spiritual life, spiritual power, and spiritual blessings – not physical prosperity (John 3:6; Romans 8:16-18; 35-38; 7:6; I Corinthians 15:22, 44; Ephesians 2:1, 5; Hebrews 9:15). In fact, Christians were promised that suffering during their earthly lives would be *normal* (Romans 5:3; I Thessalonians 3:3, 4; James 1:2-4; I Peter 2:9, 10, 21; 4:4, 12, 13; 5:8-10). Jesus, as our example, suffered; Paul and each of the other Apostles suffered; and many disciples and other believers suffered during Satan's attempt to destroy the early church. (See Appendix B for explaination.)

Our Pastor, Carl Denti, counseled with a couple who had been indoctrinated with this false doctrine:

> "A couple sought counseling after the death of their only child, a five-year-old daughter. The little girl's death was the result of a malignant brain tumor. The parents were kind, loving, warm, but unfortunately, improperly informed Christians. The couple came to me carrying an enormous burden of guilt. They believed their daughter had died because of their lack of faith. Though they had done everything a good and loving Christian parent could do for their daughter, they were overwhelmed with self-imposed blame for their child's death. The couple had sought competent medical care for their little girl, labored fervently for their daughter before the throne of grace in prayer, sought the prayers of other Christians, even brought

the elders of the church to the hospital to anoint their dying daughter with oil and pray for her healing. Though they had done all of these things, they believed they were responsible for their daughter's death.

"The reason they carried onuses of their daughter's death was because they did not have a sound Biblical perspective concerning suffering. They believed Christians suffered for only two reasons. This couple thought all Christian suffering was either the result of sin or a lack of faith. They were unfamiliar with the many passages which teach that the children of God can suffer for well doing (Psalm 119:78, 86, 161; II Timothy 3:12; I Peter 2:20). Nor were they aware of the fact that faith in Jesus Christ and a faith walk can result in affliction" (I Thessalonians 1:6; 2:14-15; Phillippians 1:30).

"Incorrect doctrine can be devastating and have a horrible effect upon one's life. I have witnessed, on more occasions than I would like to recall, how a misunderstanding or improper perspective of Christian suffering adds to the suffering of God's children. Christians can be shaken in the faith when tribulation becomes a reality. This is, in part, why Paul sent Timothy to Thessalonica and why Paul wrote his first letter to the believers in Thessalonica, so that they would not be shaken, disturbed, or moved away from the faith by suffering. Paul offers two reasons why affliction should not have shaken these Christians and leaves no room for doubting or disputing the certainty of Christian suffering."

> I Thessalonians 3:3, 4 – *That no man should be moved by these afflictions; for ye yourselves know that we are appointed to these things. For verily, when we were with you, we told you before that we should suffer tribulation, even as it came to pass, and you know.*

Obviously, mankind suffers in many ways because of his fall from innocence. However, man immediately adapts to whatever new conditions he encounters. He adjusts to the curse of a hostile environment with more clothing, to laboring for food with whistling or complaints, to difficult childbearing with heavy breathing and more complaints, to difficult children with yelling and helplessness, to battling marriages with silence and coldness, to the lost relationship with God by ignoring His existence, to the lusts of the sin nature with acceptance, to degenerative health and calamity with a superman attitude ("it will never happen to me"), and to The Final Judgment by a Just God with a Pollyanna attitude ("eat, drink, and be merry for tomorrow we shall die").

As if suffering from the loss of innocence and Paradise were not enough, mankind also fell under the direct rulership of Evil.

- **No more born as the children of God, mankind is now born into Satan's kingdom** (Colossians 1:13) under his rulership (Ephesians 2:2; 6:12), and the world's thinking systems and religions are controlled by his philosophy (Colossians 2:8; I John 5:19; Revelation 12:9).

Few people know the influence Satan and his angels (demons) have had on man throughout history. The following are some pertinent facts about his position, his authority, and his methodology:

Who Satan Is

If you picture Satan in red underwear with a pitchfork, tail, and little rubber horns, you have the entirely wrong image of him. In reality Satan is *beautiful* (Ezekiel 28:12). His name as one of the ruling angels is Lucifer, meaning day star, "son of the morning" (Isaiah 14:12); and he still appears to man today as "an angel of light" (II Corinthians 11:14).

To understand the major role Satan plays in mankind's day-to-day life, we first need to know more about his creation:

- Only God is eternal (Psalm 90:2; John 1:1; Revelation 4:8-11). He existed before and will exist after time.

- Everything else in the universe was created (brought into existence) by God (Genesis 1:2; Isaiah 40:28; 42:5; 45:12; John 1:3; Colossians 1:16; Revelation 10:6).

- All angels, including Satan, were created by God as a part of creation (Ezekiel 28:13, 15). They were *probably* created on day four of creation at the same time as the sun, moon, and stars since they are often referred to as stars (Genesis 1:16-19; 2:1, 2; Job 38:7; Isaiah 14:13, 14; Jude 13; Revelation 1:20; 12:4). The angels' abode is the heavens (Galatians 1:8; Colossians 1:16; Revelation 8:1, 2; 12:7, 8).

- The six days of creation are "the beginning" of time and are so referred to in Scripture (John 1:1, 2; Ephesians 3:9; Hebrews 1:10). All "the things" created, as referred to in Scripture, would logically include angels (Exodus 20:12; Ephesians 3:9; Colossians 1:16). There is no reason to think that angels were created prior to the beginning. Both Satan and Adam and Eve could have lived many years before their respective falls.

To understand better mankind's chief opponent, we also need to see why Satan was created and what his role is now. Knowing that Satan has authority over kingdoms, power over the elements, and superhuman strength over man is imperative in understanding human suffering. To charge God with the suffering of nations, "natural" catastrophes, wars, or a family member's sudden and "untimely" death without considering the very active part Satan plays in history is to be uninformed.

- Satan was created by God as an anointed Cherub (Ezekiel 28:14, 16). As such, Satan was to have a special role in the plan of God.

- Satan was assigned the position as Prince, or ruler, of the world – the first heavens (the atmosphere), and all of mankind (Isaiah 14:13; Ezekiel 28:14; John 14:30; II Corinthians 4:4; Ephesians 2:2). Satan made a legitimate offer to Jesus Christ when he offered Him the authority over the kingdoms of the world: (Luke 4:5, 6 – *And the devil, taking him up into an high mountain, showed unto him all the kingdoms of the world in a moment of time. And the devil said unto him, All this authority **will I give thee**, and the glory of them; **for that is delivered unto me, and to whomsoever I will I give it*** (emphasis ours).

- Logically, Satan's original role was to rule the nations with God's righteousness, justice, and mercy (all attributes of God that the Cherubim stand for); and to communicate (the job of any angel –messenger) God's Word to national leaders.

- Instead, Satan immediately (John 8:44; I John 3:8) became a liar and a murderer, at least in his heart. He fomented hatred in his heart (precursor to murder, I John 3:15) toward God for his lowly assignment; and he lied to himself about his own importance. Satan thought he should be equal to God (Isaiah 14:4) and rule angelic creation instead of, or in addition to, mankind.

- In his sinful pride, Satan rejected his earthly position and duties and said to God:

Isaiah 14:13b, 14 – *I will ascend into heaven, I will exalt my throne above the stars* (angels) *of God; I will sit also upon the mount of the congregation, in the sides of the north* (throne of God), *I will ascend above the heights of the clouds* (beyond the first heavens to the third heaven II Corinthians 12:2-4), *I will be like the Most High* (term for absolute authority).

- God answers Satan with the pronouncement of his future judgment:

Ezekiel 28:16b-17b – ***I will*** *cast thee as profane out of the mountain of God, and **I will** destroy thee . . . **I will** cast thee to the* *ground, **I will** lay thee before kings* (emphasis ours).

Isaiah 14:15a – *Yet thou shalt be brought down to sheol (hell).*

John 12:31b – *now shall the prince of this world be cast out.*

- God left Satan in his position as ruler of the world to be used to fulfill God's plan until the final judgment (John 12:31, 14:30, I John 5:19). Satan's evil is thus constantly contrasted with the goodness of God.

- Satan did ascend into the second heaven and through persuasive lies, or by his superior strength, captured one third of God's angels:

Revelation 12:4a – *And his tail drew the third part of the stars of heaven and did cast them to the earth;*

NOTE: This passage is a reference to when Satan *originally* captured one third of the angels prior to Christ's birth (Revelation 12:4-6). Satan and his angels will also wage war in heaven after the first three and one half years of Tribulation, at which time they will be cast out for good by Michael and the other angels (Revelation 12:7-9; John 12:31).

- Satan has led these fallen angles (principalities and powers) against God and man, and against God's Plan throughout human history (Matthew 12:24; 13:38-40; Mark 3:22; II Corinthians 11:13; Ephesians 6:12).

- Satan's normal modus operandi is deception the twisting of words along with an innocent appearing attitude (Acts 26:18a; Ephesians 6:11; Hebrews 2:14, 15; Revelation 12:9a; 20:3a).

- Satan also attacked mankind in the Garden. He used lies and trickery in his attempt to kill off the human race (Genesis 3:1-5). (Satan knew Adam and Eve would die if he could get them to disobey God, but he did not know God would have a plan of redemption for fallen man.)

- God then reveals to Satan who will kill him and take away his rule – the Seed of man (the Son of Man, Jesus Christ).

- Satan's main objective, from the Garden to the cross, was to prevent this One from being born into the human race. Millions of humans have suffered throughout time because of this war. Satan hates all Israel for bringing forth the Seed and all Christians for testifying of Christ. Tens of millions of Jews and Christians have suffered torture and death because of this hatred.

Conclusion

Satan has continued to be man's worst adversary as he wages his war against God. Through his attempts to consolidate governments, he causes wars which often result in starvation, illness, and other side effects. Through his rulership over the weather he can bring on any natural calamity, but only when God allows. Through his rulership over the demons he can attempt to deceive man about God through religions and false philosophies (such as psychology, humanism, or hedonism). In a variety of ways mankind suffers under the evil rule of Satan and the fallout of his battle against God.

However, Satan is not the only reason man suffers. Through sin we bring on our own suffering: *Be not deceived, God is not mocked, for whatever a man soweth, that shall he also reap* (Galatians 6:7); and, we suffer because of the sin nature of others; and, because of those things that have been cursed as a result of man's disobedience to God in the Garden. We should know that all suffering has a reason. It does not just happen: *Although affliction cometh not forth of the dust, neither doth trouble spring out of the ground* (Job 5:6). One might reasonably respond, "Well, if God is ultimately in control, why does He allow suffering at all?" We will attempt to answer that question in the next chapter.

Genesis 50:20 *But as for you, ye thought evil against me; but God meant it unto good, to bring to pass, as it is this day, to save many people alive.*

Romans 8:28 *And we know that all things work together for good to them that love God, to them who are the called according to his purpose.*

Chapter 3

WHY DOES GOD ALLOW SUFFERING?

Because man knows (or supposes that he knows) about the goodness of God, he finds unfathomable the apparently random occurrences of suffering, especially to good people. He says, "How can a loving God allow little children to starve to death," or "She was too young to die; she had not done anything to anyone," or "Everyone on board died in the plane crash – 247 people. How could it have been time for all of them?" The reasoning goes like this:

- God is love (concern for the benefit of others at a sacrificial cost to Himself). So, He would not desire for any of His creation to suffer, right? *Right*!

- God is sovereign (the absolute authority), right? *Right*! So, no subordinate member of creation can overthrow His rule, right? *Right*!

- God is omniscient (all-knowing), omnipresent (all-seeing), and omnipotent (all-powerful), right? *Right!* So, no other creature, or part of creation, can sneak up on God and get away with anything, right? *Right!*

- Then, why does suffering occur at all? *Because evil, sin, and unrighteousness exist in our world.*

The next logical question then is since these do exist, they *must* at least exist with God's permission if not His design, right? *Yes and No!*

- Yes; evil, sin, and unrighteousness exist within the overall Plan of God and by His permission, and under His restrictions. But, not by His design for God is definitely *not* the author of sin. God does not kill little babies or act unjustly toward anyone.

  James 1:13 – *Let no man say when he is tempted, I am tempted my God; for God cannot be tempted with evil, neither tempteth he any man;*

- No; God never programmed evil, sin, and unrighteousness into angels, or mankind. One third of the angels *chose* to follow Satan by the exercise of their own volition, and all of mankind are sinners in Adam and choose to confirm that position by acts of personal sin. This is possible because God's historical plan for Creation incorporates both volition *and* accountability. His sovereignty is not limited to ruling robots. God does not require that the thinking of all mankind controlled in order for Him to complete His Plan. He can integrate every right, or even wrong, decision of His creatures into His overall design and still make everything fit together perfectly.

Sin exists because God allows His creatures to make choices contrary to His desire. Satan was the first creature who chose to sin against God:

I John 3:8a – *He that committeth sin is of the devil; for the devil sinneth from beginning.*

Then, the very first human, Adam, willingly led the human race into sin:

Romans 5:12 – *Wherefore, as by one man sin entered into the world, and death by sin, and so death passed upon all men, for all have sinned.*

Rest assured, both of these decisions were within the Plan of God. The confusion about God's sovereignty comes either from **not** *rightly dividing the word of truth* (II Timothy 2:15b) or from analyzing His sovereignty from man's reasoning rather than from God's revelation.

Isaiah 55:8, 9 – *For my thoughts are not your thoughts, neither are your ways my ways, saith the Lord. For as the heavens are higher than the earth, so are my ways higher than your ways, and my thoughts than your thoughts.*

God has had a plan for human history from the beginning (creation) to the end of time (the destruction of heaven and earth, Revelation 21:1). *Nothing* has ever been allowed to interfere with God's overall Plan. Neither the will of Satan and his army of fallen angels, nor the disobedience of any person has been, or ever will be, allowed to change God's Plan in any way.

God's sovereignty has blocked every attempt by Satan and mankind to alter or to thwart His Plan for history. Man's fall in the garden, its rebellion at Babel, and the nation Israel's obsession in repeatedly following heathen gods have always been redirected by God, often by the use of force. Of course, man's fall has caused great suffering for the entire race. Similarly, Satan's consistent attempts throughout history to destroy the lineage of Jesus Christ – the Seed destined to destroy him, has always been overcome by the power and wisdom of God. Satan attempted to cause man to be destroyed in the garden; he killed Abel by his agent Cain (I John 3:12); he corrupted humanity (except Noah's family) (II Peter 2:4; Jude 6); he was behind the development of the first United Nations, Babylon; he has fomented war against Israel by many nations over the centuries; he tried to prevent the birth of Jesus Christ (Matthew 2:16; Revelation 12:7-9); and he tempted Christ to choose his rulership instead of God's (Luke 4:6, 7). Satan's attack at God's Plan has also caused much attendant suffering for mankind.

God will utilize His sovereignty to maintain His Plan – whether it is a universal flood, the hardening of Pharaoh's heart, or the blinding of Saul of Tarsus to enable him to "see the light." (It is too much aside here to illustrate the personal volitional choices each of these men was allowed to make prior to God's applying the pressure.) However, the fact that God is sovereign does not mean He will, or even can, make any decision He chooses. Each aspect of God's character (for example, sovereignty) must always function in concert with His entire character of righteousness, justice, love, etc. For instance, if God ever used His power unjustly, He would no longer be just and, therefore, no longer be God.

Summary

God did not create the sin, evil, or unrighteousness found in Satan, angels, or mankind, but allows these to exist as a part of His overall Plan for history. His omni characteristics ensure that there are no surprises to catch Him off guard. His love means that He truly cares about His creation. His sovereignty means that He can override any situation. However, God allows suffering because His Plan allows both angels and humans to make choices for which there are long-and short-range consequences.

So, why do genuinely good people suffer? Why do innocent babies starve in third world countries (and throughout rural and inner city America)? And, why do both good and bad people suffer in natural or man-made disasters? Because Satan's evil, our own sin nature, the sin expressed by others, and the repercussions of the Fall affect every area of our lives. Human suffering is simply a fact of life. Man can either curse God when he hits his thumb with a hammer, or he can take personal accountability for his own actions and accept reality as it is.

There are at least three other sources of suffering which God allows. They are self-induced, specialized, and indirect suffering.

Self-Induced Suffering

God also allows suffering as the natural consequences for breaking His standards or laws which are designed to bring order to the physical universe. The example of the thumb being hit by a hammer is an illustration of the physical law that *two objects cannot occupy the same space simultaneously.* It teaches the lesson, "Pay attention to what you are doing!"

God's laws for proper sexual relationships within a committed husband/wife marriage are being violated by fornication, adultery, and homosexual acts throughout the world today with the dire results of broken homes and displaced children plus the spread of AIDS and other highly contagious and painful diseases. (Romans 1:24-27; I Corinthians 7:1-3; Hebrews 13:4). God does not need to punish each offender personally; He pre-assigned the penalty when He established the law.

God's laws for fair business dealings between people establishes a basis for trust. When these laws are broken, innocent people are hurt (Leviticus 19:11, 35, 36; Proverbs 11:1; 16:11; James 5:4-6).

Even the laws given by God to govern interpersonal relationships have consequences when broken. For instance, *love thy neighbor as thyself* (Leviticus 19:18b and James 2:8b) is not only God's law but also just good common sense. Eventually there will be a pay-off for wrongful treatment of others.

The basic law for raising responsible children is for parents to train them into obedience and respect for authority (Exodus 20:12; Ephesians 6:2, 3; Colossians 3:20a). We have experienced three or four generations of untrained children in this country. The nation, the parents, and the children all suffer because of this lawbreaking. Mankind suffers when any of the hundreds of other beneficial standards given by God are broken. Cain, first son of Adam and Eve, is a perfect example. God clearly told him that his bloodless sacrifice of fruit was totally unacceptable and gave him another chance. But Cain, angry with God for not accepting his choice of offering (the *works* of his hands), murdered Abel. The resulting curse was truly a self-induced punishment (Genesis 4:3-14).

Specialized Suffering

There are times in history when God calls on a special person to suffer as an illustration or proof of His Plan or Character. Job, of course, is such an example; so also was the beggar, congenitally blind until Jesus cured him (John 9:1-35, especially verse 3); and Lazarus in his death (John 11:1-44, especially verse 4); and Jesus' undeserved death on the cross (Luke 23:44-46; Romans 5:17; I Peter 3:18). All of the apostles, except John, suffered violet deaths, as did thousands of Christians who died horribly in the Roman arenas. Their martyrdom is what helped spread Christianity throughout the world. Still today there are Christians who are persecuted and even die for their faith in Jesus Christ.

Indirect Suffering

When God punishes a nation or an individual for violation of His laws, individuals innocent of that particular wrongdoing suffer at least partially from the fallout. For instance: a man who cheats or steals from his employer will cause his whole family to suffer at some point; a nation, like Germany, that severely hurts God's special people, the Jews, was virtually annihilated, causing many non-guilty Germans and others to suffer indirectly. Parents who break their marriage covenant by divorce, cause indelible and painful damage to their children. When Jacob showed favoritism to Joseph, it resulted in pain for Joseph, all of his brothers, as well as for Israel (Genesis 37:3, 4).

The life of Corrie Ten Boom is an example of both direct and indirect suffering.

> "On December 28, 1944, after ten months of incarceration in concentration camps, Corrie Ten Boom was free. She had lost her father and beloved sister to the horrors of Nazi death camps. Gaunt, filthy, and weak, Corrie made her way to the railway station and boarded a train for a three-day journey home to Holland.
>
> "The Ten Booms, all devout Christians, had provided a hiding place in their home for persecuted Jews during World War II. Corrie, who was fifty-nine at the time of her arrest, was placed in an isolation cell for the first few weeks of her imprisonment. Depression and the struggle to maintain a sense of hope consumed her.
>
>> " 'Only to those who have been in prison does freedom have such great meaning. When you are dying - when you stand at the gate of eternity - you see things from a different perspective than when you think you may live for a long time. I [stood] at the gate for many months, living in Barracks 28 in the shadow of the crematorium.' "
>
> "Corrie vowed if God allowed her to live, she would tell as many people as possible about the love and forgiveness of Jesus Christ. She also promised to go wherever He led. She miraculously obtained a small New Testament from a prison worker and smuggled it past guards.
>
>> "Before long we were holding clandestine Bible study groups for an ever growing

group of believers, and Barracks 28 became known throughout the camp as 'the crazy place, where they hope.' "

"For the next four decades following her release from prison, Corrie traveled extensively, speaking in more than sixty countries, captivating audiences with her inspiring faith and love for God. She is the author of nine books, one of which is *The Hiding Place*, a personal account of her arrest and time spent in prison. She also produced five films.

"God has plans - not problems - for our lives. Before she died in the concentration camp in Ravensbruck, my sister Betsie said to me, 'Corrie, your whole life has been a training for the work you are doing here in prison - and for the work you will do afterward.'

"The life of a Christian is an education for higher service. No athlete complains when the training is hard. He thinks of the game, or the race. (Romans 8:18-23)

> "Looking back across the years of my life, I can see the working of a divine pattern which is the way of God with His children. When I was in a prison camp in Holland during the war, I often prayed, 'Lord, never let the enemy put me in a German concentration camp.' God answered no to that prayer. Yet in the German camp, with all its horror, I found many prisoners who had never heard of Jesus Christ."
>
> " 'If God had not used my sister Betsie and me to bring them to Him, they would never have heard of Him. Many died, or

were killed, but many died with the name of Jesus on their lips. They were well worth all our suffering. Faith is like radar which sees through the fog - the reality of things at a distance that the human eye cannot see.' "
© In Touch Ministries® ITM, Inc.

Conclusion

Rather than thinking that suffering is the abnormal condition of man, it should be easy to see that it is normal. Simply stated, mankind suffers because it is mankind:

> Job 14:1 – *Man that is born of a woman is of few days, and full of trouble.*

> Psalm 39:4, 5 – *Lord, make me to know mine end, and the measure of my days, what it is, that I may know how frail I am. Behold, thou hast made my days as an handbreadth, and mine age is as nothing before thee. Verily every man at his best state is altogether vanity. Selah.*

> Ecclesiastes 2:23a – *For all his days are sorrows, and his travail grief;*

With the reality of these verses in mind, the next chapter examines the various ways that man's mind attempts to cope with the inevitable.

Mankind's Distress

Suffering from Satan's warfare

Suffering from self-depravity

Suffering from the sin natures of others

Earth

Suffering from breaking universal laws

Suffering from consequences of the Fall

Figure 3.1

Mankind is surrounded with causes for his suffering. It is a burden too heavy to bear without God.

Job 13:15a *Though he slay me, yet will I trust in him;*

Isaiah 26:3, 4 *Thou wilt keep him in perfect peace, whose mind is stayed on thee, because he trusteth in thee. Trust ye in the Lord forever; for in the Lord God is everlasting strength.* (See also Psalm 46:1-3; 56:3, 4)

Chapter 4

HOW MAN FACES SUFFERING

The chart on the previous page is a reminder of a popular joke circulating thirty or forty years ago. Notice that the arrows on this chart surround the one isolated man. The joke starts off with the Lone Ranger and Tonto being totally surrounded by an angry band of hostile Indians. The Lone Ranger said, "What are we going to do, Tonto?" Tonto, his faithful Indian sidekick, responded, "What do you mean, *we*, pale face? In other words, man exists surrounded and all alone in a dangerous and menacing world. How has he coped with this plight down through the centuries?

Man's Solutions

(See if you can identify yourself.)

1. Most people pretend evil does not exist. They block out the reality of death and major suffering, over which they have no control.

Proverbs 28:26a – *He that trusteth in his own heart is a fool*, (See also Job 15:31.)

To pretend nothing bad will happen when a person steps on a plane, drives freeways, or lives in crime-ridden cities is the ostrich approach to life. When it prevents man from properly maintaining his car, or preparing for retirement or for his eternal destiny, this approach is foolish.

2. Self-sufficient people stubbornly try to handle most suffering in their own strength and wisdom.

Isaiah 5:21 – *Woe unto them who are wise in their own eyes, and prudent in their own sight!* (See also Psalm 20:7, 8; 33:16-19; Proverbs 3:5; Isaiah 47:10.)

These are people who are too proud to turn to anyone else for help, including God. By their intelligence and their extreme self-discipline, they attempt to make it through life's problems.

3. Insecure people usually seek sympathy from others. A classic example might be those who always seek the strength of individuals or groups instead of turning to God.

Psalm 146:3 – *Put not your trust in princes, nor in the son of man, in whom there is no help.* (See also Isaiah 31:1; Jeremiah 17:5.)

These poor little ones were probably trained in childhood into thinking they could never do anything right on their own and so always needed someone to do their thinking for them. God intends that all men and women find their strength only in Him.

4. The supermen/women laugh at danger and intentionally gamble with death, injury, or financial ruin.

Luke 6:25b – *Woe unto you that laugh now! For ye shall mourn and weep.* (See also Job 18:7; Psalm 80:6; Proverbs 14:9; Jeremiah 17:5; I Peter 1:24.)

5. The rich and/or elite are inclined to believe that their wealth or position will protect them.

James 1:11 – *For the sun is no sooner risen with a burning heat, but it withereth the grass, and its flower falleth, and the grace of the fashion of it perisheth; so also shall the rich man fade away in his ways.* (See also Psalm 49:6-13; Isaiah 5:22; Ephesians 5:18; I Timothy 6:17.)

It is no surprise that Jesus said, *a rich man shall with difficulty enter into the kingdom of God* (Matthew 19:23b). Wealth and status can become an obsession which obscures man's need for God until it is too late. (See Luke 16:20-31.)

6. People of weak character often try to run from suffering by avoiding reality through alcohol, drugs, or even self-induced insanity.

Proverbs 20:1 – *Wine is a mocker, strong drink is raging, and whosoever is deceived thereby is not wise.* (See also Isaiah 5:22; Ephesians 5:18.)

7. Strong-willed people knowingly rebel against God, choosing immorality and/or idolatry for their religion.

Isaiah 42:17 – *They shall be turned back, they shall be greatly ashamed, that trust in carved images, that say to the melted image, Ye are our gods.* (See also Romans 1:19-32.)

These people want something to believe in, but they reject God (*will not* submit) and invent a god that they control. They will often pray (make wishes on) a symbol (cross, ankh, animal) rather than submit to the real God to whom they must be accountable.

8. Aesthetic people are more prone to turn to religion whereby they attempt to earn God's approbation by their good deeds (law keeping, helping others, self-sacrificing).

Luke 18:9 – *And he spoke this parable unto certain who trusted in themselves that they were righteous, and despised others.* (See also Acts 9:5 cf. 26:5; Luke 6:1-7; 18:10-14; Romans 2:1-8; II Corinthians 10:12; Philippians 3:9.)

Specifically, many religious people today truly believe that keeping the Ten Commandments will provide them with prosperity, health, and God's acceptance. In their imagination such people have established a god who is pleased with their offerings (their deeds can be truly good or just fluff).

Almost all of the world's religions attract these hypercritical, self-deluded people.

Summary

As we have just seen, the indomitable nature of mankind has devised a variety of ways to deal with things his mind chooses not to face – such as major suffering and death. He can just pretend the evil does not exist, trust in his own strength, rely on the sympathy of others, laugh at danger, depend on his position of wealth, turn to some form of sublimation, invoke his strong will, or turn to some religion to make it all go away. Of course, none of these attempts will make suffering go away or even lessen it.

On the other hand, some Christians know how to turn to God for the real strength and upholding needed to deal with the most severe tests of life. These believers actually accept life, and suffering, and death as reality and turn to the revealed God of Scripture (the Lord God, Jehovah Elohim, Savior God, Messiah, Jesus Christ).

> Psalm 25:20 – *Oh, keep my soul, and deliver me; let me not be ashamed; for I put my trust in thee.*
>
> Proverbs 3:5 – *Trust in the Lord with all thine heart, and lean not unto thine own understanding.*
>
> John 16:33 – *These things I have spoken unto you, that in me ye might have peace. In the world ye shall have tribulation: but be of good cheer; I have overcome the world.* (See also Job 5:19-22; I John 2:14; 5:4, 5.)

Hebrews 13:5, 6 – *Let your manner of life be without covetousness, and be content with such things as ye have; for he hath said, I will never leave thee, nor forsake thee. So that we may boldly say, The Lord is my helper, and I will not fear what man shall do unto me.*

The following true-life story exhibits this type of trust:

"Horatio G. Spafford, a forty-three-year-old Chicago businessman, suffered financial disaster in the Great Chicago Fire of 1871. He and his wife were still grieving over the death of their son shortly before the fire, and he realized they needed to get away for a vacation. Knowing that their friend Dwight L. Moody was going to be preaching in evangelistic campaigns in England that fall, Spafford decided to take the entire family to England. His wife and four daughters went ahead on the SS *Ville du Havre*, and he planned to follow in a few days.

"But on the Atlantic Ocean the ship was struck by an iron sailing vessel and sank within twelve minutes. Two hundred and twenty-six lives were lost – including the Spaffords' four daughters. When the survivors were brought to shore at Cardiff, Wales, Mrs. Spafford cabled her husband, 'Saved alone.'

"Spafford booked passage on the next ship. As they were crossing the Atlantic, the captain pointed out the place where he thought the *Ville du Havre* had gone down." That night Spafford wrote the beautiful hymn, *It Is Well with My Soul*. One of the verses of that hymn is, *When sorrows like sea billows roll . . . it is well, it is well with my soul."* *

This type of internal strength, security, comfort, and peace of soul is not possible apart from a deep relationship with God. Since this is the only effective way to approach death and suffering, this proven method of success will be the focus of the next section.

* *The One Year Book of Hymns,* 1995, Tyndale House Publishers, Wheaton, IL.

Psalm 27:1 *The Lord is my light and my salvation; whom shall I fear?*

II Timothy 1:7 *For God hath not given us the spirit of fear, but of power, and of love, and of a sound mind.*

Chapter 5

Fear Of Death And Dying

It has been said that we begin to age the day we are born. Actually our physical body is developing throughout our childhood until we reach full growth at about twenty-seven years old. Then our body begins to deteriorate at an ever-increasing rate until it just "gives out." This assumes we do not die prematurely from disease, self-abuse, accident, crime, etc.

Although every one of us realizes the truth of our mortality, we often avoid facing the inevitable. And yet our lives are like a vapor.

Facing Death

The recorded history of man is approximately 6000 years. Your life expectancy is about 1 1/2% of that period – a speck in time.

Psalm 144:4 – *Man is like to vanity; his days are like a shadow that passeth away.* (See also Psalm 103:15, 16.)

Much more important, the entire 6000 years of recorded history, compared with eternity, is virtually nonexistent:

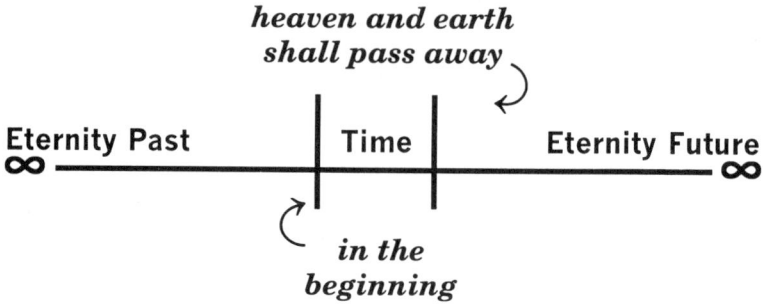

Figure 5.1

However, every human soul was designed by God to live *forever*.

Genesis 2:7 – *And the Lord God formed man of the dust of the ground, and breathed into his nostrils the breath of life; and man became a living soul* (literally an always living soul). (Emphasis ours.)

I Corinthians 15:45a – *And so it is written, The first man, Adam, was made a living soul* (literally an always living soul). (Emphasis ours.)

Since the soul lives forever, it is infinitely more important that man concern himself with his soul's eternal life than his short physical life. The suffering of the eternal soul damned to the lake of fire will be much worse than any physical suffering or death any man has ever experienced in time.

Matthew 16:26 – *For what is a man profited, if he shall gain the whole world, and lose his own soul? Or what shall a man give in exchange for his soul?*

Matthew 25:41 – *Then shall he say also unto them on the left hand, Depart from me, ye cursed, into everlasting fire, prepared for the devil and his angels;*

I Peter 4:18 – *And if the righteous scarcely be saved, where shall the ungodly and the sinner appear?*

Revelation 20:15 – *And whosoever was not found written in the book of life was cast into the lake of fire.*

A real passenger on the Titanic, about whom we never hear, understood the body and soul issue perfectly well. He willingly gave up his physical life to save the souls of others who would die that day. His name was John Harper. He was a Scottish minister who was traveling on the Titanic to preach at the Moody Church in Chicago. Harper gave his life jacket to another man and then was seen swimming from one passenger to another, pleading with them to accept Christ. Only six of the 1500 people struggling in the water after the ship sank were later rescued. One young man "had climbed up on a piece of debris. Harper, who was struggling in the water near him, shouted out, 'Are you saved?' 'No,' the man replied. Harper then shouted the words from Scripture: *'Believe on the Lord Jesus Christ and thou shalt be saved.'* The man did not answer, and a moment later he drifted away on the waves.

"A few minutes later, the current brought the two men back together. Again Harper asked, 'Are you saved?' Once again, the answer was, 'No.' With his dying breath, Harper shouted, *'Believe on the Lord Jesus Christ and thou shalt be saved.'* Harper then slipped under the waves for the last time.

Then and there, the man to whom he had witnessed decided to turn his life over to Christ. Four years later, at a Titanic survivors' meeting in Ontario, Canada, this man tearfully gave his testimony recounting how John Harper had led him to the Lord."

> *The Titanic's Last Hero*, Olive Press, 1997

People are concerned too much with what others will say or think instead of fearing the Almighty God. They should fear the only one (God) who has the power to destroy both body and soul in hell, not the ones (men and Satan) who can only destroy the body in time.

> Matthew 10:28 – *And fear not them who kill the body, but are not able to kill the soul; but rather fear him who is able to destroy both soul and body in hell.*

Satan was never given authority to judge anyone to hell, the ultimate punishment.

> Hebrews 9:27 – *And as it is appointed unto men once to die, but after this the judgment.* (See also Revelation 14:7; 20:16.)

But wait! Why should you believe that a loving God would destroy His own creation?

1. Because God will not spare Satan and the angels who rebelled against Him (Matthew 25:41).

2. Because God has not spared and will not spare those angels who attempted to debase the lineage of Jesus Christ (Genesis 6:4-7; II Peter 2:4; Jude 6).

3. Because God has already set the penalty for man's disobedience resulting in man being dead (spiritually), dying (physically), and damned (soul). (See pages 8-10.)

4. And, because God did not spare His own Son the agonizing death on the cross and all of His suffering leading up to that death.

II Corinthians 5:21 – *For he hath made him, who knew no sin, to be sin for us, that we might be made the righteousness of God in him.*

It is only this sin-free sacrifice that can save the soul of man.

I Corinthians 15:22 – *For as in Adam all die, even so in Christ shall all be made alive;*

Hebrews 10:39 – *But we are not of them who draw back unto perdition, but of them that believe to the saving of the soul.*

I Peter 1:9 – *Receiving the end of your faith, even the salvation of your souls.*

Jesus Christ, the Son of God, has provided the path for man's salvation. That path is very narrow. *And they said, believe on the Lord Jesus Christ, and thou shalt be saved,* (Acts 16:31a).

> John 5:24 – *Verily, verily, I say unto you, He that heareth my word, and believeth on him that sent me, hath everlasting life, and shall not come into judgment, but is passed from death unto life.* (See also John 3:15-18.)

It is not the humanity of a historical Jesus Christ that must be believed (even Satan knows Christ exists); it is faith in the person of Jesus Christ – His deity and His work.

> John 14:6 – *Jesus saith unto him, "I am the way, the truth, and the life; no man cometh unto the Father, but by me."*

Faith, believing, is the means of accepting God's Word as real. If you believe that Jesus Christ is God, that Christ died and was resurrected on your behalf, that you are dead in Adam's sin (plus your own personal sins), then there is nothing left for you to do but accept Christ's gift of salvation and eternal life *right now*!

> Ephesians 2:8, 9 – *For by grace are ye saved through faith; and that not of yourselves, it is the gift of God – Not of works, lest any man should boast.*

When you simply believe in Christ, your soul is saved, delivered, redeemed, eternally alive. Your body will be resurrected after death (Romans 8:23; I Corinthians 15:49, 52), and you are already spiritually alive (John 3:6, 7; Ephesians 2:5). Praise God!

Facing Dying

Now that we have dealt with the eternal suffering of the soul, we can deal with the mental anguish man experiences in time concerning death. There are two aspects of death which can cause suffering: fear of the process of dying, and fear of the afterlife. For the true Christian, the one who has accepted Christ as his Savior, there should be absolutely no fear of the afterlife. He or she should be able to say as Paul did, *For to me to live is Christ, and to die is gain* (Philippians 1:21).

However, the unbeliever faces the hereafter with a certain amount of apprehension. He has heard quotes from the Bible about a final judgment and about heaven and hell. Since his best hope is that it is just a story, he chooses not to face the issue at all. If Satan wanted to keep man in this gullible state, he might try to convince man that there really is no heaven or hell, no afterlife, and definitely no punishment. Of course, then man would not need Christ at all. There would be no need for the passages God gave to man:

> I Corinthians 15: 54b-57 – *Death is swallowed up in victory. O death, where is thy sting? O grave, where is thy victory? The sting of death is sin; and the strength of sin is the law. But thanks be to God, who giveth us the victory through our Lord Jesus Christ.*

Obviously, in Satan's war against God and man he needs to burn, discredit, or otherwise keep the Bible away from man. I believe he has been at work to do this partly through seemingly innocent entertainment.

You have probably noticed the onslaught of movies and TV shows over the past ten or fifteen years depicting a painless, "have it your way" after-death experience. *Cocoon* found such acceptance with its 1985 release that *Cocoon 2* came out in 1988. *Ghost* and *Ghost Dad* followed shortly on the heels of their success. TV shows like *Sightings* and *Unsolved Mysteries* have paraded supposed near-death and reincarnation experiences for the last decade. Would it not be nice if all death were accompanied by floating off into the light with a warm, fuzzy feeling? And, how about the thought that there will be no judgment and no literal hell? I am sorry, but you will just have to adjust to reality; it will not adjust to your fantasies.

How about the mental suffering man experiences when he faces his fear of dying? Man does not fear death nearly so much as he does the process of dying. The point of death, or just after, is an abstract thought and cannot be compared with anything ever before experienced. However, everyone fears the process of dying, particularly in a specific manner that can be imagined – such as drowning, burning alive, suffocating by being buried alive, helplessly falling, being mangled in a plane, train, or auto crash, or stumbling into a den of snakes or deadly insects. It is not the moment life is over that causes terror but the fear of the minute or minutes before that moment. And Satan has always held mankind in slavery by its fear of this dying process.

> Hebrews 2:14b-15 – *that through death he might destroy him that had the power of death, that is, the devil, And deliver them who, through fear of death, were all their lifetime subject to bondage.*

What is truly amazing to the author is that it is easier or more palatable for man to "have faith" in a movie fairy tale like *Cocoon* than it is to "have faith" in the historically real Jesus Christ.

Some day *you will die*! How you face dying and the afterlife is your choice. You will either face eternity as a believer, trusting God to comfort you during the process of dying, as well as trusting in His plan for eternity; or, you can remain in bondage to Satan and his delusion that although dying is too terrible to consider, your afterlife *might be* okay in spite of what the Bible says.

> John 3:36 – *He that believeth on the Son hath everlasting life; and he that believeth not the Son **shall not see life, but the wrath of God abideth on him***. (Emphasis ours)

If you still have not made this most important decision of your life, there probably would be no point in your completing this book. From this point on, the presentation will be only for those who are true believers. Suffering for the unbeliever has already been covered, and his only course of action is to "grin and bear it." For the believer, God has prepared everything necessary to overcome this life, our death, and the life hereafter. Therefore, a Christian's course of action is to trust in the completed provision of God.

> John 14:24 – *Peace I leave with you, my peace I give unto you; not as the world giveth, give I unto you. Let not your heart be troubled, neither let it be afraid.*

The next section will reveal how a believer can grow in his knowledge of God's character, and his experience in God's power to the point of being victorious over the effects of suffering, thereby glorifying God.

SECTION TWO

ARE CHRISTIANS DIFFERENT?

*Psalm 37:7 Rest in the Lord,
and wait patiently for him;
fret not thyself because of him
who prospereth in his way,
because of the man who bringeth
wicked devices to pass.*

*Romans 8:31 What shall we then
say to these things? If God be for us,
who can be against us?*

Chapter 6

CHRISTIANS ARE PEOPLE, TOO!

Some Christians think they are above the problems of unbelievers. They believe they can control the lusts of the flesh (or will not even be tempted any more), or that they are immune from the influence of Satan, or that they are beyond physical or emotional pain, or that it will be no problem to love their neighbor as they do themselves. If you are under any of these delusions, this chapter is for you. But, be encouraged. Even though Christians face each of the following curses, they have something the unbeliever does not have – *spiritual power*.

Curse One – The Sin Nature

Oh, how I wish God had taken my sin nature from me at the point of salvation (or today would still be fine). No longer to have the pride of self importance, no longer to lust to indulge physical appetites, no longer to be enticed away from a life not pleasing to God would be a blessing. As the Apostle Paul said, *O, wretched man that I am!*

who shall deliver me from the body of this death? (See Romans 7:14-25.)

Yes, dear brother or sister, Christians, just like unbelievers, are cursed with a sin nature which is driven by each person's own particular lusts:

> James 1:14 – *But every man is tempted, when he is drawn away of his own lust, and enticed.*

Spiritual Power: God the Holy Spirit, a member of the triune Godhead, indwells every believer:

> I Corinthians 6:19 – *What? Know ye not that your body is the temple of the Holy Spirit who is in you, whom ye have of God, and ye are not your own?*

> Galatians 5:16, 17 – *This I say then, Walk in the Spirit, and ye shall not fulfill the lust of the flesh. For the flesh lusteth against the Spirit, and the Spirit against the flesh; and these are contrary the one to the other, so that ye cannot do the things that ye would.* (See also Romans 7:18, 25b; Ephesians 2:2.)

The Holy Spirit is a miraculous gift for the Christian. The Old Testament Jews had nothing like it except The Law, which was powerless to prevent sin, it only defined it. The Christian has an indwelling power from God that exceeds the power of the sin nature and enables the believer to rule lusts! *Walk in the Spirit, and ye shall not fulfill the lusts of the flesh.*

Curse Two – Satan

Christians suffer as do non-Christians because Satan is still the ruler of this world (Ephesians 2:2). As such, he influences government leaders (Revelation 20:3), creates false philosophies (Colossians 2:8), and uses unbelievers to oppose God's gospel message (John 8:44; II Corinthians 4:4; I Timothy 4:1-2; I Thessalonians 2:18). For instance, Satan is behind all false philosophies that are against God and/or the Bible. Examples: Humanism, Theologies that teach works for salvation, Evolution, Situation Ethics, etc. These philosophies govern the entertainment industry as seen by its consistently showing Bible-believing characters as being mentally deranged, lecherous, or greedy. Obviously, the producers have a systematic view (philosophy) against the Bible and any who believe it to be the truth. This may even explain their numerous misquotes such as "cleanliness is next to Godliness" or "God helps those who help themselves," (neither of which appear in the Bible) plus the constant misapplications of passages out of context which produce negative or false impressions of God, the Bible, or Christianity.

Let me testify that Satan is truly active in the lives of Christians today.

> "I've never seen Satan; I'm hardly important enough. But, I have encountered Satan's agents on several occasions. They have always enticed me to stop what God was leading me to do in exchange for instant wealth or being a knight in shining armor for a damsel in distress.
>
> "The first time was when God led me to leave a great position to work with a pastor friend for no pay. The company offered me a 40% pay

increase plus to pay for a Pepperdine Master's Degree if I would stay – a powerful enticement for a high school graduate. I saw the writing on the wall and politely rejected the fabulous offer. The second time was just after I had completed writing *What the Bible Says About . . . Child Training* and giving live seminars all over the country. A young married woman who had been attending my Bible class asked for marriage counseling. She flattered my manhood and I enjoyed being thought of as wise, compassionate, and stable. I proudly thought I could objectively handle her devotion; however, my continued counseling with her got me emotionally involved with her life. I never felt that this girl was a conscious agent of Satan, but I do believe that Satan was attempting to destroy my marriage and ministry through her deep psychological needs. *Finally*, I applied the Biblical teaching to abstain from all appearance of evil (II Thessalonians 5:22) and moved my faithful wife and me one thousand miles away. God has obviously honored this commitment to my wife over the balance of our lives together. We have grown closer in our relationship than ever before the incident, and it made Virginia's book, *On the Other Side of the Garden*, a living testimony for her."

J. Richard Fugate

Spiritual Power: When a believer is faced with Satan's deceit, he has access to spiritual power which can enable him to handle the curse:

> Ephesians 6:11 – *Put on the whole armor of God, that ye may be able to stand against the wiles of the devil.*

I John 4:4 – *Ye are of God, little children, and have overcome them, because greater is he that is in you, than he that is in the world.*

Knowledge of the Word of God is the power to defeat Satan. (see Chapter 11).

Curse Three – Physical and Emotional Problems

Like any unbeliever, Christians are subject to hereditary deficiencies, accidents, and high stress – all of which produce physical and/or emotional suffering. If you prick Christians, do they not bleed? In other words, Christians are not immune from anything the unbeliever has to deal with in the body, including death. Believers can and do suffer from diseases, viruses, accidents, diabetes, heart failure, depression, and any other malady common to man.

> "Should the Lord tarry and I live more than threescore and ten, and if medical science does not make any further advancements in the area of vision, there is a possibility that my vision may become radically impaired. My grandfather was afflicted with severe cataracts and had several operations. However, by the time he departed from his body, his eyesight still was very poor. My dearly beloved grandmother, who is well into her eighties, has a similar problem. She is no longer able to read print, and that includes her large print Bible, because her eyes have failed. As for myself, I cannot see across the room without my glasses, and I have to remove them in order to read. Should I live long enough, it is likely that I will experience a problem similar to my grandparents. If the time

comes when my vision would be so impaired as not to be able to read and study the Word of God, I would consider myself sorely afflicted. That condition would be a source of severe tribulation to me. However, I know that even then I can trust in God to have a plan for my continued life. Should this occur, the cause of the affliction would be my genetic connection to my grandparents and ultimately my genetic link to Adam. It would be the result of being a member of Adam's race, which is one of the reasons believers experience tribulation."

Carl Denti

Spiritual Power: Believers can turn to a God who cares about their sufferings when they face physical and emotional problems.

> 2 Samual 22:3 – *The God of my rock; in him will I trust: he is my shield, and the horn of my salvation, my high tower, and my refuge, my savior; thou savest me from violence.*
>
> Romans 8:26 – *Likewise, the Spirit also helpeth our infirmity; for we know not what we should pray for as we ought; but the Spirit himself maketh intercession for us with groanings which cannot be uttered.*
>
> Hebrews 4:15 – *For we have not an high priest who cannot be touched with the feeling of our infirmities, but was in all points tempted like as we are, yet without sin.*

Curse Four – Other People

Christians suffer just as do unbelievers because of other people and their sin natures. People are difficult to live with. Contrary to Satan's false philosophy that man is mostly good and occasionally does wrong, the truth is that man is basically evil and will occasionally do that which is right – often for some self-benefiting reason.

When a non-Christian (or even a Christian who possesses the Spirit of God but thwarts God's power by personal sin) is your spouse, your relative, or anyone else with whom you must associate, there will be suffering for you.

Adam suffered because of Eve (Genesis 3:6), mankind suffered because of Adam (Romans 5:12), Abel suffered because of Cain (Genesis 4:8), Hagar suffered because of Abraham and Sarah (Genesis 16:1-6), and on down to you who may have suffered because of someone else's sin.

Believers must be well-versed in the Word of God to deal with the curse of *other people* and their sin natures. The books of Psalms and Proverbs can teach a believer wisdom about people and how to deal with them.

> Hebrews 4:12 – *For the word of God is living, and powerful, and sharper than any two-edged sword, piercing even to the dividing asunder of soul and spirit, and of the joints and marrow, and is a discerner of the thoughts and intents of the heart.*

Spiritual Power: The believer, filled with the Holy Spirit of God and mature in the knowledge of God's Word, is well prepared to deal with these problems that are common to man. The bottom line is that Christians are *potentially* much better off than unbelievers who must deal barehandedly with the curses against humanity. We say *potentially* because having access both to the power of the Holy Spirit and the Word of God is not the same as utilizing them. Immature believers (those not knowledgeable of Scripture) or carnal believers (those who have unconfessed sin in their lives, thus quenching the Holy Spirit) are still powerless to deal with any obstacles. Please study the following chart:

A 10,000 Watt appliance plugged into a 220V socket

Mature believer who posesses a maximum knowledge of God's Word (Romans 12:2)	who is SPIRITUAL (filled with the Holy Spirit - Galations 5:16)	Produces both types of God's power (Ephesians 3:20)

A 10,000 Watt appliance with the cord disconnected

Mature believer who posesses a maximum knowledge of God's Word (Romans 12:2)	who is CARNAL (has unconfessed sin in the life - I John 1:6-10)	Split-souled person - unstable, insecure, mixes human thinking and Scripture together (James 1:8)

A 1 Watt bulb glowing as brightly as it can

Immature believer (newborn or one who has regressed - I Corinthians 2:14; Hebrews 5:12)	who is SPIRITUAL (filled with the Holy Spirit - Galations 5:16)	Has good intentions, but does not know what to do or how to do it (I Corinthians 13:11)

A 1 Watt bulb - cold and dark

Immature believer (newborn or one who has regressed - I Corinthians 2:14; 3:3) Hebrews 5:12)	who is CARNAL (has unconfessed sin in the life - I John 1:6-10)	Has no power. Looks and acts like an unbeliever (I Corinthians

Figure 6.1

Hebrews 13:5b *for he hath said, I will never leave thee, nor forsake thee.*

Hebrews 13:6 *So that we may boldly say, The Lord is my helper, and I will not fear what man shall do unto me.*

Chapter 7

CHRISTIANS ARE SPECIAL PEOPLE

God calls Christians, *a people of His own.*[1] The single Greek word translated into that phrase in the following verse literally means "make a circle around; acquiring or making an acquisition." It refers to God laying a claim on the Gentiles to be the nation He appointed to take Israel's place for a specified period of history as the chosen race.

> I Peter 2:9 – *But ye are a chosen generation, a royal priesthood, an holy nation, a people of his own, that ye should show forth the praises of him who hath called you out of darkness into his marvelous light;*

Praise God! You belong to Him and He cares what happens to you:

> Romans 8:14 – *For as many as are led by the Spirit of God, they are the sons of God.*

> Hebrews 4:16 – *Let us, therefore, come boldly unto the throne of grace, that we may obtain mercy, and find grace to help in time of need.*

> I Peter 5:7 – *Casting all your care upon him; for he careth for you.*

God calls Christians His children. The Greek word translated "children"[2] in the following verse means progeny, member of the family.

> Romans 8: 16-17a – *The Spirit himself beareth witness with our spirit, that we are the children of God; And if children, then heirs – heirs of God, and joint heirs with Christ.*

Christians are also called sons.[3] This Greek word emphasizes the Christian's relationship as a natural or legally adopted member of the family:

> Hebrews 12:5b – *My son, despise not thou the chastening of the Lord, nor faint when thou art rebuked of him*; (See also vv. 6-8.)

God has made believers spiritually alive with the new ability to understand spiritual things as taught by the (Holy) Spirit of God:

> Romans 8:15 – *For ye have not received the spirit of bondage again to fear; but ye have received the Spirit of adoption, whereby we cry, Abba, Father.*

Christians Are Special People

> I Corinthians 2:11 – *For what man knoweth the things of a man, except the spirit of man which is in him? Even so the things of God knoweth no man, but the Spirit of God.*

On the other hand, the natural man cannot discover or understand the spiritual things of God:

> I Corinthians 2:14 – *But the natural man receiveth not the things of the Spirit of God; for they are foolishness unto him, neither can he know them, because they are spiritually discerned.*

Spiritual life is given to each believer at the point of his or her salvation, and this allows fellowship with God through the Holy Spirit (I Corinthians 2:12-14). The "spirit of adoption" by which Christians become legitimate children of God, coheirs with Jesus Christ, and able to comprehend spiritual things as taught by God the Holy Spirit, is called the "Spirit of Christ."

> Romans 8:9 – *But ye are not in the flesh but in the Spirit, if so be that the Spirit of God dwell in you. Now if any man have not the Spirit of Christ, he is none of his.* (See also Romans 8:15; Galatians 2:20; 4:6, 19; Ephesians 3:17a; Colossians 1:27.)

The Spiritual Difference

Although Christians are just people who are subject to suffer from the same sources unbelievers do, *everything about suffering changes for them*:

II Corinthians 5:17 – *Therefore, if any man be in Christ, he is a new creation; old things are passed away; behold, all things are become new.*

Although the believer will still suffer from his sin nature, from Satan's control of the world, from normal physical and emotional problems, and from other people, these are *old things* and for him *all things become new.*

While life just happens to the unbeliever, the believer understands the curse on man and has the source of spiritual power to deal with it. While suffering before salvation warns man of his frail humanity and the justice to come, after salvation suffering is controlled by our loving Father who has new objectives for a believer's suffering, such as:

- Tests for spiritual growth
- To glorify God
- To be a testimony for Jesus Christ
- As examples for other believers
- Chastisement for rebellion
- Proof of faith
- Promise of eternal life and glory

I Peter 4:13 – *But rejoice, inasmuch as ye are partakers of Christ's sufferings, that, when his glory shall be revealed, ye may be glad also with exceeding joy.*

Remember, Christians belong to God and are His special people. He will never test His own beyond their ability to pass.

> I Corinthians 10:13 – *There hath no temptation taken you but such as is common to man; but God is faithful, who will not permit you to be tempted above that ye are able, but will, with the temptation, also make the way to escape, that ye may be able to bear it.*

Summary

You may have come from the most dysfunctional home ever imagined. Your father may have ignored you for years. Your mother may not have accepted a single thing you did as being right. But you now have a Spiritual Father who has made you special. You are His possession and He accepts you as His child, even His heir. He has given you spiritual life that so you can share in His wisdom as taught by God the Holy Spirit while here on earth. However, if you are going to be successful in handling the tests and tribulations of the Christian life to the glory of God, you must be trained! Praise God from Whom all blessings flow.

> "Frances Ridley Havergal, writer of music, poems, and devotionals in the 1800's, wrote *Kept for the Master's Use* and *The Overflowing Life*. When she was in physical weakness and in pain she could say gladly: "How infinitely blessed it is to be *entirely* Christ's. To think that you and I are never to have another care or another fear, but that Jesus has undertaken simply everything for us! And isn't it grand to have the privilege of being His instruments? It does seem such loving condescension that He should use us. Pain, as to God's own children, is, truly and really, only blessing in disguise. It is but His chiseling, one of His graving tools, producing the likeness to Jesus

for which we long. I never yet came across a suffering (real) Christian who could not *thank* Him for pain!"

They Found The Secret,
Zondervan Publishing, 1984

Footnotes

[1] Greek, *peripoiesis*, "literally, to make a circle around – as around a possession; an acquisition."

[2] Greek, *teknon*, "child; specifically descendant; natural progeny."

[3] Greek, *huios*, "son; legitimate son (even if adopted)."

Psalm 37:40 *And the Lord shall help them, and deliver them; he shall deliver them from the wicked, and save them, because they trust in him.*

Psalm 130:5 *I wait for the Lord, my soul doth wait, and in his word do I hope.*

Colossians 1:28 *Whom we preach, warning every man, and teaching every man in all wisdom, that we may present every man perfect in Christ Jesus.*

Chapter 8

ALL GOD'S CHILDREN NEED TRAINING

Every believer begins the Christian life with a newborn spirit which is immature concerning spiritual things:

- A Christian's spiritual life begins as his physical life began – as a newborn baby.[1]

    I Peter 2:2 – *As newborn babes, desire the pure milk of the word, that ye may grow by it.*

- Naturally this baby is spiritually immature in speaking, understanding, and thinking. The word translated "child"[2] in this next passage literally means "immature."

I Corinthians 13:11 – *When I was a child, I spoke as a child, I understood as a child, I thought as a child; but when I became a man, I put away childish things.*

- God's objective for your spirit is maturity –to learn the full knowledge of the Son of God. (*But we have the mind of Christ,* I Corinthians 2:16b; *Let this mind be in you, which was also in Christ Jesus,* Philippians 2:5.)

Ephesians 4:13 – *Till we all come in the unity of the faith, and of the knowledge[3] of the Son of God, unto a perfect man, unto the measure of the stature of the fullness of Christ*; (See also Colossians 1:28; 4:12; James 1:4.)

I Timothy 2:4 – *Who will have all men to be saved, and to come to the knowledge[3] of the truth.*

Ephesians 4:13; Colossians 1:28, 4:12; and James 1:4 each contain a Greek word translated "perfect."[4] Biblically, it means "the state of being mature" (ripe or complete). God's Word refers to believers as being either spiritually immature or mature. (Compare Ephesians 4:13 with 14 and Hebrews 5:13 with 14.)

NOTE: Please understand, this is not a discussion of the believer's gradual development through varying stages of his Christian walk. That never-ending development utilizes spiritual maturity, plus reliance on the Holy Spirit, plus trust in God on a day-by-day basis. Obviously, a believer can be completely mature in knowledge and yet act against that knowledge – Abraham, Eli the priest, and

David, for example. Therefore, spiritual maturity is only an attainable state of knowing God's Word, not a guarantee of *acting mature* at any one moment. Spiritual maturity is more of a *preparation* for Christian living than an end in itself (I Corinthians 8:1). For example: the process of boot camp will result in some recruits becoming marines – they either pass or they do not. However, each marine's performance in action determines his stage of development (rank).

Just as children are reluctant to do their schoolwork and chores, immature believers are also stubborn about learning God's Word. Immaturity always questions the need for learning: "What good will it be." "I won't need it." "It's too hard, time consuming, or dry." So, God helps His children, as we help our children. He may chastise (the intentional infliction of pain for the purpose of correction), or control (the restriction or application of pressure), or test (challenging to cause the right choice to be made). Most of these corrective actions will be in the form of suffering. It will be up to us to learn how to identify God's gentle touch and then to make an adjustment, when that is necessary.

How Do God's Children Learn?

When God established Israel as a nation, He commanded the parents on how to train up their children.

> Deuteronomy 6:6-7 – *And these words, which I command thee this day, shall be in thine heart; And thou shalt teach them diligently unto thy children, and shalt talk of them when thou sittest in thine house, and when thou walkest by the way, and when thou liest down, and when thou risest up.*

This same concept exists with immature Christian converts as well:

> Matthew 28:19-20a – *Go ye, therefore, and **teach** all nations, baptizing them in the name of the Father, and of the Son, and of the Holy Spirit, **Teaching** them to observe all things whatsoever I have commanded you;* (Emphasis ours.)

Spiritual maturity is obviously attained by means of learning the Word of God (Romans 12:2, *renew your mind;* Ephesians 4:13, *knowledge of the Son of God*; Colossians 1:28, *teaching every man in all wisdom*). Note especially:

> Hebrews 5:12 – *For when for the time ye ought to be teachers, ye have need that one teach you again the first principles of the oracles of God, and are become such as have need of milk, and not of solid food.* (Milk equals baby food; strong meat equals food that requires adult teeth to eat.)

Coming to know God's Will is also dependent on our knowledge of Scripture:

> Romans 12:2 – *And be not conformed to this world, but be ye transformed by the renewing of your mind, that ye may prove what is that good, and acceptable, and perfect, will of God.*

Notice, there are no passages teaching that a believer will know God's Will or learn spiritual maturity by means of emotional experiences, observing rituals, or premature ministry. Just like salvation, spiritual growth *must* come by grace, not by works.

Galatians 3:3 – *Are ye so foolish? Having begun in the Spirit, are ye now made perfect by the flesh?* (See also Galatians 3:1-5.)

Teaching Our Children

"My wife and I decided in 1971 to move away from society, out into the mountains of Colorado, and become self-sufficient. We also decided to home school our three children. It was somewhat of a traumatic year for our oldest daughter (13) since she was required *to learn* everything she covered for the first time in her life. (Her English teacher had told her just to skip over any word she couldn't read; so she was skipping more than one half of her 7th grade reader!)

"In the full spirit of family revival, I started teaching a mandatory family Bible study every morning before school. We started off studying the character of God and then went to other basic doctrines. For children thirteen, nine, and seven years of age, they listened attentively, but we never knew what they had actually learned. That was twenty-seven years ago. They have each said that year was a turning point in their commitment to God.

"Our oldest daughter was witnessing to her Catholic father-in-law one day and realized that she was drawing upon memories of those lessons her dad had taught her. Later she said, 'Dad, I could hear you speaking as I spoke.' And, when her son died in her womb just weeks before he was due to be born, trust in the love of God bore her through the terrible pain and sorrow. Later when she and her husband were able to adopt an eighteen-month-old baby boy (who was approximately the same age her son would have been), she was able again to praise God for His mercy and His grace. Doctrine must be learned *prior* to Satan's attack in order for the believer to be able to stand. (Ephesians 6:11-13)."

J. Richard and Virginia Fugate

Enter the Adversary

Satan hates God's Word. He attempts to prevent souls from coming to salvation by stealing away the Gospel:

> Mark 4:15 – *And these are they by the wayside, where the word is sown; but when they have heard, Satan cometh immediately and taketh away the word that was sown in their hearts.*

I believe that Satan works on the mentality (heart) of the hearer by spreading doubt, such as: "I am too evil to be saved," or "Just believing is surely not enough; I must change my life or do some good work in addition. After all, you don't get something for nothing in life." This poor soul would have heard the Word, but would not have accepted it.

For just this reason, God sent Paul to the Gentiles:

> Acts 26:18 – *To open their eyes, and to turn them from darkness to light, and from the power of Satan unto God, that they may receive forgiveness of sins, and inheritance among them who are sanctified by faith that is in me.* (See also Matthew 13:19-23; cf. Luke 8:11-15.)

Satan changes tactics if he is unable to prevent a person's salvation. Next he attempts to disqualify or destroy immature believers.

> I Peter 5:8 – *Be sober, be vigilant, because your adversary, the devil, like a roaring lion walketh about, seeking whom he may devour.* (See also I Timothy 3:6, 7; II Timothy 2:26.)

Satan attacks the naive believer with his subtle tactics. He first causes the believer to *doubt* in God's Word; second, to feel *discontent* with God's provision; and third, to have *disbelief*, thereby leading the believer to rebellion (Genesis 3:1-6).

Every new baby believer is born onto battlefield Earth where Satan is attempting to conquer God and/or to destroy His Plan with his agents.

> Acts 13:10 – *And said, O full of all deceit and all mischief, thou child of the devil, thou enemy of all righteousness, wilt thou not cease to pervert the right ways of the Lord?* (See also Matthew 4:1-11; 16:23; John 13:2; II Corinthians 2:11; I Thessalonians 2:18; I Timothy 5:15.)

If not protected, the defenseless baby can become engaged in full-time spiritual warfare without the knowledge of how to defend himself or how to utilize the spiritual weapons God has provided for this battle. His natural response would be to turn to his own natural (fleshly) abilities to save himself.

Wrong!

This is a spiritual child of God, one who is to share in the inheritance of eternal life and is meant to live out this life by means of spiritual power. God desires that all believers become mature in the Word and live by the power of the Holy Spirit.

> Galatians 5:25 – *If we live in the Spirit, let us also walk in the Spirit.* (See also Proverbs 3:5; Galatians 3:3; Ephesians 6:11-12; Philippians 2:13.)

Without a doubt, Scripture makes it perfectly clear that *God does not want or need human works.* God's Plan is for Him to provide man's salvation and spiritual life. Power for this spiritual life is provided in two types – dynamic power through the indwelling Holy Spirit, and operating energy through knowing the Word. The statement, "God helps those who help themselves," is false philosophy out of the pit of hell. The Bible nowhere says or even implies this concept. Instead, God desires for His people to rest in His work. The following verses portray that fact:

> Exodus 14:13a, 14 – *And Moses said unto the people, Fear not, stand still, and see the salvation of the Lord which he will show to you today, . . . The Lord shall fight for you, and ye shall hold your peace.*

> Isaiah 40:31 – *But they that wait[5] upon the Lord shall renew their strength; they shall mount up with wings like eagles; they shall run, and not be weary; and they shall walk, and not faint.*

Philippians 2:13 – *For it is God who worketh in you both to will and to do of his good pleasure.*

Hebrews 4:9-10 – *There remaineth, therefore, a rest to the people of God. For he that is entered into his rest, he also hath ceased from his own works as God did from his.*

God does not desire strong men or women. He desires to empower those who are weak and those who voluntarily submit their strength to Him. "God finally found in me a believer weak enough to use" is a quote attributed to the China missionary, Hudson Taylor.

II Samuel 22:2-3a – *And he said, The Lord is my rock, and my fortress, and my deliverer, The God of my rock; in him will I trust*[6]

Job 13:15a – *Though he slay me, yet will I trust*[7] *in him;*

Psalm 37:5 – *Commit thy way unto the Lord; trust*[8] *also in him, and he shall bring it to pass.*

Psalm 91:4a – *He shall cover thee with his feathers, and under his wings shalt thou trust;*[6]

Proverbs 3:5 – *Trust*[8] *in the Lord with all thine heart, and lean not unto thine own understanding.*

Proverbs 28:26a – *He that trusteth*[8] *in his own heart is a fool,*

Isaiah 26:3 – *Thou wilt keep him in perfect peace, whose mind is stayed on thee, because he trusteth[8] in thee.*

Matthew 26:39b – *. . . O my Father, if it be possible, let this cup pass from me; nevertheless, not as I will, but as thou wilt.*

I Corinthians 1:27b – *. . . and God hath chosen the weak things of the world to confound the things which are mighty;*

II Corinthians 12:9 – *And he said unto me, My grace is sufficient for thee; for my strength is made perfect in weakness. Most gladly, therefore, will I rather glory in my infirmities, that the power of Christ may rest upon me.*

Summary

Baby Christians must be trained or they will be casualties in Satan's warfare. They must be taught the Word of God and must be taught to depend on the Power of God (the Holy Spirit). They also need to learn how to utilize God's power by setting aside their own physical strength, wisdom, and intellectual ability.

A study of how to grow in God's power will be presented in the next three chapters. Suffering can be understood, tolerated or, conquered and utilized to the benefit of the believer and the glory of God with mastery of this knowledge.

Footnotes

1 Greek, *brephos*, "infant; a totally dependent child."

2 Greek, *nepios*, "immature; state of being childish."

3 Greek, *epiginosko*, "to know completely, or through and through; above or beyond simple recognition or understanding."

4 Greek, *teleios*, "mature; full grown, ripe; state of being fully complete or developed."

5 Hebrew, *qavah,* "sure expectation" faith/trust built on weaving together of past trusts fulfilled, fourth in the hierarchy of Hebrew words for trust.

6 Hebrew, *chasah,* "trust; to take temporary refuge" refuge, as under a rock. This word is second in the trust words, above only, *aman*, the word for "simple belief; or to acceptance as true.'

7 Hebrew, *yachal*, "trust, in time of maximum pressure; total confidence." Fifth (or top) in the hierarchy of Hebrew words for trust.

8 Hebrew, *batach*, "trust; total dependence." Third of the Hebrew words for trust.

Isaiah 46:9 *Remember the former things of old; for I am God, and there is none else; I am God, and there is none like me.*

Mark 12:32 . . . *for there is one God, and there is no other but he.*

Chapter 9

BELIEVER TRAINING 101

Who Is God?

Understanding the character of God is the first step in knowing and trusting Him. God does not expect a blind (unknowing) faith from His people. This is why He has made Himself known to man throughout history by His deeds (creation, Exodus deliverance, the miracles of Jesus) and His recorded Word: John 20:31a – *But these are written, that ye might believe that Jesus is the Christ, the Son of God; and that believing ye might have life through his name.*

When you learn and accept (believe) that God is love, you will actually know that He has your best interests in mind through any suffering you must experience. When you learn and believe that God is omniscient, omnipresent, and omnipotent, you will know that He is capable of either delivering you from any trial you must face or empowering you to handle it to the glory of God. When you learn and believe that God is righteous and just, you will truly know that He will always be fair to you, even though you may be suffering in an unfair situation at the time. When you learn and believe that God is eternal, absolute truth, and never changing, you can completely rest in His plan and His promises. When you learn and believe that God is sovereign, you will know that He is always in control of *everything* that affects your life – He can even override physical laws and Satan's rulership on earth.

Caution: God is not a one-dimensional person who can operate according to a single aspect of His character to the exclusion of any or all of His other aspects. This is the integrity of God – His complete character held in tension. For example, God cannot exercise justice against anyone without considering His righteousness and His love – so there is no reason to fear an arbitrary or capricious judgment from God. Likewise, God will not allow His love to override or compromise His character of righteousness and justice so there is reason to fear God's righteousness or justice for those who are unrepentant concerning their wrongdoing.

The following chart is an overview of the most commonly accepted characteristics of God's essence:

The Multifaceted Character of God

THE ATTRIBUTES OF GOD	MEANING

I. Sovereign (Absolute authority)

Daniel 4:35 – And all the inhabitants of the earth are reputed as nothing; and he doeth according to his will in the army of heaven, and among the inhabitants of the earth, and none can stay his hand, or say unto him, What doest thou? (See also Ex. 8:10; 9:14; Deut. 4:39; II Chron. 20:6; Ps. 83:18; 115:3.)	No Power (authority or might) can prevent God from fulfilling a plan or a promise He has made. With God there is no curruption of power because of the integrity of his character

II. Righteous (Standards based on a just measure)

Psalm 145:17 – *the Lord is righteous in all his ways, and holy in all his works.* (See also Ezra 9:15; Ps. 7:9; 48:10; 119:137; Jer. 23:6)	God is one ruler who will *never* require His subjects to do anything self-destructive, or unfair to anyone else.

III. Just (Completely fair)

Deut 32:4 – He is the Rock, his work is perfect; for all his ways are justice a God of truth and without iniquity, just and right is he. (See also Lev. 19:35, 36; Ps. 19:137; Prov. 16:11 Is. 45:21b; Dan. 4:37; Rev. 15:3)	God defines justice as that which is right, correct, fair, as in using honest scales and the same weights for buying and selling. Justice in consideration of people is to deem poor and rich, ill and well, to be equal.

THE ATTRIBUTES OF GOD	MEANING
IV. **Perfect Love** (Sacrificial Love)	
I John 4:7-10 – *Beloved, let us love one another; for love is of God, and everyone that loveth is born of God, and knoweth God. He that loveth not knoweth not God; for God is love In this was manifested the love of God toward us that God sent his only begotten Son into the world, that we might live through him. Herein is love, not that we loved God, but that he loved us, and sent his Son to be the propitiation for our sins.* (See also Rom. 5:8; Gal. 5:22; Eph. 2:4; 3:19; 5:2; I Jn.. 3:16; 4:16, 19.)	God is love (I Jn. 4:16b). The Greek word always used to express God's love as a part of His character is *agape*. This word indicates: [1] a reaching out to help one who does not care, does not know his need, or is even an enemy. [2] requires a sacrifice (personal cost) on the part of the donor. [3] is for the benefit of the recipient. [4] never has a charge for the recipient to pay. [5] 1 Cor. 13:4-8a give characteristics of Christian love.
V. **Veracity** (Absolute truth)	
Titus 1:2 – *In hope of eternal life, which God, who cannot lie, promised before the world begun.* (See also Psalms 33:4; 146:6; Isa. 65:16a: Jn. 14:17; 17:17; Rom. 3:4a; Hb. 16:18.)	What can we say? God cannot tell a lie, a half-truth, or a misleading statement. He can refuse to answer for a number of reasons, but He will not lie. Satan is the father of lying. (Jn. 8:44b).

THE ATTRIBUTES OF GOD	MEANING
VI. Omnipresent (All-present)	
Proverbs 15:3 – *The eyes of the Lord are in every place, beholding the evil and the good.* (See also Job 28:24; 42:2; Ps. 139:7-12; Is. 66:1; Is. 66:1; Jer. 23:24; Heb. 4:13.)	God has no restrictions of presence. He can simultaneously be in Heaven, on Earth at multiple locations, in the sea, within peoples minds, anywhere and everywhere.
VII. Omniscient (All-knowing)	
Rom. 11:33 – *Oh, the depth of the riches both of the wisdom and knowledge of God! How unsearchable are his judgements, and his ways past finding out.* (See also Ps. 44:21; 94:11; 139:4; 147:5; Prov. 2:6; 3:19; Is. 55:9.)	All that can be known has always been known by God. And, His knowledge and wisdom are far beyond man's ability to comprehend. Through His word, He gives man information beyond the physical universe.
VIII. Omnipotent (All-powerful)	
Matthew 19:26 – *But Jesus beheld them, and said unto them, Withmen this is impossible; but with God all things are possible.* (See also I Chron 29:12; Job 42:2; Ps. 106:8; Lk. 1:37; Rom 13:1; Eph. 1:21.)	God, as the Creator, is above all authority or ruling power that He allows, more powerful than any creature that He empowers with a portion of His might.

THE ATTRIBUTES OF GOD	MEANING
IX. Immutable (Unchangeable)	
Num. 23:19 – *God is not a man, that he should repent. Hath he said, and shall he not do it? Or hath he spoken, and shall he not make it good?* (See also Heb. 1:12; 13:5b, 13:8; James 1:17b.)	Unlike all false gods man has worshipped throughout history, *The God* never changes, His criteria for dealing with man never changes – good and evil never change, that which God accepts or rejects from man remains the same.
X. Eternal (Timeless life)	
Revelation 1:8 – *I am Alpha and Omega, the beginning and the ending saith the Lord, who is, and who was, and who is to come, the Almighty.* (See also Psalms 9:7; 90:4; 145:13; Isa. 43:13; Lam. 5:19; I Tim. 1:17.)	God Existed — God Exists — God Keeps Existing ∞————————————∞ TIME

Chart 9.1

In order to receive the full benefit from this chart, we suggest that you study each characteristic and carefully read the verses given. Then consider and write down how each of God's characteristics applies to your trust in Him.

The Psalmists seldom fail to remember and mention one or more of God's attributes when praying for His current blessing or deliverance. See the following Psalms for examples:

- Psalm 2 – omnipotence
- Psalm 3 – love
- Psalm 4 – omnipresence, love, omnipotence
- Psalm 5 – omnipresence, righteousness, justice
- Psalm 6 – love, omnipresence
- Psalm 7 – justice, righteousness
- Psalm 8 – sovereignty, omnipotence
- Psalm 9 – justice, love
- Psalm 10 – righteousness

Likewise, Christians would do well to praise the demonstration of God's character during their prayers that they have seen in theirs and other's lives.

Psalm 18:30 *As for God, his way is perfect; the word of the Lord is proved; he is a shield to all those who trust in him.*

Romans 5:3, 4 *And not only so, but we glory in tribulations also, knowing that tribulation worketh patience; And patience, experience; and experience, hope;*

Chapter 10

BELIEVER TRAINING 201

Trusting in God

Nothing will carry the believer through the pain, waiting, and loneliness of suffering better than totally trusting in God. Even the baby believer can commit to memory some basic verses on trusting in God. Verses like: *And we know that all things work together for good to them that love God* (Romans 8:28a); or, *Casting all your care upon him; for he careth for you* (I Peter 5:7) can be utilized in times of emergency. However, for major suffering in duration or intensity, a believer will also need to know about the character of God and/or the deeper concepts behind these and other verses in their category.

Christians must accept the fact that suffering is integral to every believer's faith in God: *In this ye greatly rejoice, though now for a season, if need be, ye are in heaviness through manifold trials* (I Peter 1:6). As believers face ever-increasing temptations and tests in their lives, they progress in the need for ever-higher levels of faith: *For in it is the righteousness of God revealed from faith to faith; as it is written, The just shall live by faith* (Romans 1:17).

Note that the Romans 5:3 and 4 passage at the beginning of this chapter reveal that intense suffering produces patience (endurance), and patience (without whining) produces proven results, and proven results produce confidence (in God).

Hebrew Words For Trust

As we suggested in the footnotes of a previous chapter, there are five different Hebrew words for faith (or trust) used in the Old Testament. We suggest that those words represent different levels of trust which a believer can progress through as he experiences God's deliverance from suffering in his life. There is no provable correct sequence for these five words except by interpretation based on human logic. I have chosen to list them in decending order from what I believe to be the highest level of trust on the following chart:

Translated word emboldened	Hebrew word
Job 13:15 – *Though he slay me, yet will I **trust** in him;*	***yachal*** (total confidence) "trust during times of maximum pressure."
Job 14:14 – *If a man die, shall he live again? All the days of my appointed time will I **wait**, till my change come.*	***qavah*** (expectation) "sure expectation"

Brokerage IRA Client Agreement

Note for Massachusetts Residents

The following disclosures apply to Massachusetts residents only:

1. **General Disclosure Statement.** Any documentation provided to me that inc[...] admissible as evidence of such transfer and shall constitute prima facie proc[...]

   The initiation by me of certain electronic fund transfers from my account w[...] effectively eliminate my ability to stop payment of the transfer.

   Unless otherwise provided in this Disclosure, I may not stop payment of elec[...] electronic access for purchases or services unless I am satisfied that I shall no[...]

   No interest is paid on the cash balance in my account. Dividends, at a rate th[...] account. I may terminate this Agreement by notifying you in writing.

   If a problem or error with respect to my account concerns a transfer to or from [...] investigation may be limited to a review of your own records. If you decide th[...] to pursue the matter further.

   If I comply with the conditions set forth above, in cases in which I think that a [...] was not authorized to initiate any transfers from my account, you will request [...]

Psalm 25:3 – *Yea, let none that **wait** on thee be ashamed; let them be ashamed who transgress without cause.*

Psalm 62:8 – ***Trust** in him at all times, ye people; pour out your heart before him. God is a refuge for us. Selah.*

batach (dependence) "trust"

Psalm 91:2 – *I will say of the Lord, He is my refuge and my fortress, my God; in him will I **trust**.*

Psalm 7:1 – *O Lord my God, in thee do I put my **trust**; save me from all those who persecute me, and deliver me.*

chasah (trust) "temporary trust; take refuge."

Psalm 37:40 – *And the Lord shall help them, and deliver them; he shall deliver them from the wicked, and save them, because they **trust** in him.*

Genesis 15:6 – *And he **believed** in the Lord; and he counted it to him for righteousness.*

aman (believe) "to believe (or accept) as truth"

Chart 10.1

Aman in Hebrew represents the beginning step of believing. Simply believing in Christ's substitutionary death on the cross results in the believer's deliverance from the suffering of damnation. *Believe on the Lord Jesus Christ, and thou shalt be saved* (Acts 16:31b).

Before continuing, there is need to clear up some confusion about the concept of faith. Faith is simply the means for accepting as reality any information that your soul (your immaterial essence of mentality, emotion, and will) has determined is true (whether it is true or not). Anyone can believe a lie.

Example: I see an old, wooden bridge on the road ahead; so I park and investigate its physical condition, the possible danger (how deep the canyon is), and finally decide I can TRUST in its strength, based on my empirical and rational analysis. However, my wife remains emotionally unsure. She can imagine the car going through the old planks and sees little kids strewn about on the rocks below. She can't BELIEVE in this bridge. About that time a logging truck weighing five times our weight, barrels down the road and flies across the bridge as it obviously had done many times before. Now, my wife can also BELIEVE and we cross the bridge without incident. Notice: The bridge did not support our car because of our faith, but because it was well constructed. The strength of trust, faith, or belief is always in the *object*, not in the *subject*.

Of course, faith in spiritual truths **cannot** be discerned without God the Holy Spirit revealing it to a spiritually animated person (I Corinthians 2:11-14). *Now faith is the substance of things hoped for, the evidence of things not seen* (Hebrews 11:1). Or, more literally, "Faith is the reality of things being expected, proof of matters not visible."

Faith is similar to swallowing. Have you ever taken a bite of something that tasted terrible and you immediately spit it out? You rejected, or did not accept, that bite. On the other hand, you normally swallow any bite which tastes and feels right to you. Likewise, you believe (accept) information which seems right to your soul. There is no merit in believing. Obviously, any merit is in the **object of belief** rather than for the one merely accepting, or swallowing, what has been presented to him.

Peitho is the root noun in the Greek for all of the New Testament's faith words: to believe, to be a believer, to hold a belief, to trust, etc. It is important to realize that every word in this family **must** have an external object on which to act intellectually. If you "believe," it is always "in something." If you "have faith," that faith is always "in something specific." If you are "a believer," it is always "in a person, or an object, or a body of information." You must seek out the object of faith every time you see faith/believe words in the Bible. It would be more accurate to coin these words "faithin," "believein," and "trustin." EXCEPTION: The noun form of *peitho, pistew,* is often used technically with its article to mean "The Faith," standing for the entire realm of doctrine known, such as:

> Ephesians 4:13 – *Till we all come in the unity of **the faith**, and of the knowledge of the Son of God, unto a perfect man, unto the measure of the stature of the fullness of Christ* (our emphasis).

Chasah is the next level of faith on the chart of Hebrew words for *trust*. This word represents safety to one needing refuge. It was used to describe a rabbit ducking under a rock when chased by a predator. Almost any believer will cry out to God in a crisis, and God's deliverance will build that believer's trust in Him. Keep in mind that each of these words for faith is God's provision for a believer's physical, mental, or emotional suffering. God never means to imply that His provision eliminates a believer's pain altogether, but that He will enable you to handle it if it remains. When the Fugates gave their ten-year-old son regular shots for his terrible allergies, they used to say, "Be brave, son." After several months of this he said, "I am being brave, but it *still* hurts." He thought that being brave meant he would not feel the pain. He then learned that being brave was the courage to handle the pain.

Batach is shown as the Hebrew word for the third level of faith. This word meant to transfer your heavy load onto another to carry for you. *Cast thy burden upon the Lord, and he shall sustain thee; he shall never suffer the righteous to be moved* (Psalm 55:22). Some believers will utilize this level, but it means setting aside the pride one has in his own self-reliance – "I don't need anyone to help me; I can do it myself!" Relying on God's power rather than taking the glory for self in the flesh is difficult for many people.

Quavah is shown as the Hebrew word for the fourth level of *faith*. This word signified a heavy rope made out of strands of twine twisted together. The believer who has trusted God consistently at the other levels now possesses the memory of a strong rope of trust woven out of the protection and deliverance he has experienced. It is not that the believer **possesses** more faith; it is that God has demonstrated more of His character in which to trust. At this level a believer has sure expectation that God will protect him or deliver him as needed, even if the test is undisclosed at the time (as with Noah). Very few Christians reach this level of trust in God. It seems that most Christians would rather fight their battles in their own strength and lose than to let go and let God – and win.

Yachael is the Hebrew word for the final level of *trust*. Job was not the only believer to experience this level. Read *Foxe's Book of Martyrs* to see how thousands of Christians throughout history have trusted in God, even unto death. We cannot help wondering how many of today's Christians would evidence such trust.

> A girl only six weeks old lost her sight because of a doctor's error. Tragic, undeserved suffering, you say? How could anyone trust in a God who would allow such a terrible thing to happen? This girl became the inspirational hymn writer, Fanny Crosby (1820-1915). She once said about her blindness, "I have always believed that the good Lord, in His infinite mercy, by this means consecrated me to the work that I am still permitted to do." Some of her doctrine-filled hymns are *All the Way My Savior Leads Me, Close to Thee*, and *To God Be the Glory*.

Conclusion

The prayer of the writer of this book is that all readers will see whatever suffering they must face as a means of experiencing God in their lives on a very personal basis.

Colossians 1:9, 10 *For this cause we also, since the day we heard it, do not cease to pray for you, and to desire that ye might be filled with the knowledge of his will in all wisdom and spiritual understanding; That ye might walk worthy of the Lord unto all pleasing, being fruitful in every good work, and increasing in the knowledge of God:*

Chapter 11

BELIEVER TRAINING 301

Knowing God

It is probably beginning to dawn on most who have persevered to this chapter that the Christian life is not a bed of roses. Believers can revel in these facts: *O death, where is thy sting? O grave, where is thy victory?* (I Corinthians 15:55) and, *The Lord knoweth how to deliver the godly out of temptations, and to reserve the unjust unto the day of judgment to be punished* (II Peter 2:9). However, life on Earth may be very difficult, especially in progressing toward becoming a Christian soldier. This is a spiritual warfare, not a fleshly one. Human intelligence, physical might, and a scintillating personality are totally worthless in this battle. Believers must set aside all human abilities and . . .

> Ephesians 6:11, 12 – *Put on the whole armor of God, that ye may be able to stand against the wiles of the devil. For we*

> *wrestle not against flesh and blood, but against principalities, against powers, against the rulers of the darkness of this world, against spiritual wickedness in high places.*

The song from "Man of La Mancha" sums up the spiritual soldier's sentiments:

> *To fight for the right without question or pause, to be willing to march into hell for a heavenly cause!*

If a believer is going to be in battle and even suffer, let it be for a reason that can be understood and one that is much more important than for temporal, self-centered benefits.

God is *very* serious that all believers become spiritually knowledgeable, which requires learning God's Word from cover to cover. Does this seem that God is asking too much? Consider that a doctor, or a lawyer, or a CPA will attend college six years or more, become familiar with hundreds of books on his subject, and perhaps even become an expert in one facet of his field. Even a high school dropout can become interested in model planes, auto repairs, fly fishing, the Internet, or whatever and devour hundreds of magazines (and maybe a book or two) on his chosen subject. However, if you tell a believer (especially male) that God expects him to read, learn, and know *one* special book – the Bible, only 1300 to 1400 pages long – that man may begin to give you all of the reasons why he could not manage that gargantuan feat in a lifetime.

This one book is more important to your life than all of the other books combined. Dedicate yourself to a year-through-the-Bible reading schedule and a walk-through-the-Bible content study. Make sure that you are attending a Bible-teaching church that teaches God's grace rather than man's works. And then be ready for an accelerated training course. God will allow you to be tested concerning your total dependence on Him for every step forward of your spiritual preparedness.

Onward, Christian Soldier!

Every Christian starts his spiritual life as an immature infant. This life begins at his birth at the cross (John 3:6, 7).

Chronological Age	State of Being
(*Brephos*) "infant" – unable to care for self	(*Nepios*) "immature; childish"

A believer can remain spiritually immature throughout his chronological Christian life. He can be a temper-throwing child; a rebellious teen; or a resentful, self-excusing, blaming-everyone-else adult. There is no Scriptural reference to one being "childish plus" or "almost mature." As the man said, "either you is, or you ain't," referring to being either spiritually mature or immature.

The opposite of becoming a knowledgeable Christian soldier is to remain ignorant, cannon fodder for Satan, or even worse, to become one of his dupes.

> I Timothy 3:6 – *Not a novice, lest being lifted up with pride he fall into the condemnation of the devil.* (See also II Timothy 2:26; I Peter 5:6-10.)

The characteristics of the spiritually immature believer are easy to detect. They are: limited knowledge resulting in instability; foolishness; being easily deceived and led astray; having childish speech, thinking, and reasoning (I Corinthians 3:1; 13:11; Ephesians 4:14; Hebrews 5:11-13).

On the other hand, a believer can dedicate himself to learn the Word of God – to become a mature man[1] (Ephesians 4:14; James 3:2). Spiritual maturity is intended by God to become *every* believer's normal state (I Corinthians 14:20; Ephesians 4:14; Philippians 3:15; Colossians 1:28; 3:10; 4:12; James 1:4; Hebrews 5:12-14; 6:1). Spiritual maturity is the basis for soul stability, skill in living (wisdom), and effective service (Romans 12:1, 2).

> **NOTE:** Spiritual maturity is not equivalent to the Christian Walk. Spiritual maturity consists only of mastering the knowledge of God's Word. The Christian Walk incorporates all of the aspects of a believer's Christian existence as it varies from day to day. These include:
>
> - Spiritual maturity.
> - Walking in the Holy Spirit.
> - Submission of personal will to God's will.
> - Utilization of Spiritual gift.
> - Walking by faith.

The Christian Walk is described as being a walk "in the Spirit" (Galatians 5:16); "in newness of life" (Romans 6:4); "in good works" (Ephesians 2:10); "worthy" (Ephesians 4:1); "in love" (Ephesians 5:2); "in light" (Ephesians 5:8); "as wise" (Ephesians 5:15); "worthy, fruitful, increasing in knowledge" (Colossians 1:10; "in

Christ" (Colossians 2:6); "in wisdom" (Colossians 4:5); "in honesty" I Thessalonians 4:12); "in light" (I John 1:7); "in Christ" (I John 2:6); "in truth" (II John 4).

While spiritual maturity is an absolute state, the Christian Walk is the never-ending, living experience of Christianity.

These two dissimilar concepts could be charted thus:

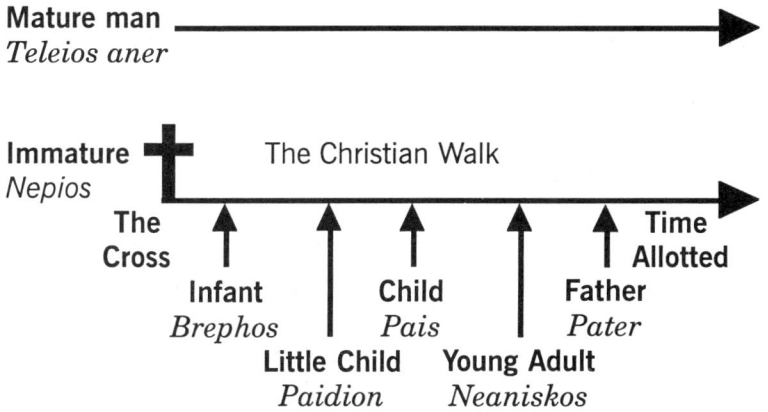

Chronological Development

NOTE: Emboldened words are English; non-emboldened words beneath are transliterations of the Greek.

In this chart, the bottom line represents a person's time line – the number of years God has allotted to him. The cross represents the moment one personally accepts Christ as his Savior and his spiritual life begins. The Chronological Development indicates the different stages of the Christian life. The believer is either spiritually mature or immature while he attempts to live the Christian Walk.

Suffering as it Relates to Spiritual Maturity

It seems that the tests, trials, and chastisements the Lord lovingly allows into believers' lives cause them to remember Him, need Him, and turn to Him. When comfortable, healthy, and prosperous, the tendency is to forget about God. In many cases, it is the one suffering the most and the longest who has the most intimate relationship with God and Jesus Christ. Here is an example from our family.

> "After several years of illness, our youngest daughter, JoAnn, was diagnosed with Lupus at 28 years old. Her firm trust in God's character before her diagnoses carried her through the very tough years of questions-without-answers, and now her trust in the Lord carries her through the unknown future as well. Her faith continues to grow each day as evidenced by this excerpt from a letter.
>
> *'Dear Mom and Dad, I believe this last year has been a great growing time for me spiritually. I have learned so much about leaning on the Lord, patience, and grace. I've learned more about the love of God and the sacrifices that He has made for all believers and I am beginning to appreciate more and more what Christ has done for me.'"*
>
> "This letter was written while she was suffering from inflammation around her heart that kept her almost completely bedridden for three months. The following letter was written in 1999 after another serious illness and after having been almost completely house bound for about two years:

> 'I wonder what it will be like without pain, though I'm beginning to think of it as my friend for it draws me closer to Him. I know how weak I am and am not confident that I would be so occupied with my Lord if I didn't need Him so.'"
>
> J. Richard & Virginia Fugate

Just as any student is tested on each new level of knowledge studied, a believer will be tested as he learns each new concept in the Bible. God's assurance is that the test will not be beyond a believer's ability to endure:

> I Corinthians 10:13 – *There hath no temptation taken you but such as is common to man; but God is faithful, who will not permit you to be tempted above that ye are able, but will, with the temptation, also make the way to escape, that ye may be able to bear it.*

The attitude a believer has when tempted is part of the test. Most of these tests will take the form of suffering and/or the need to trust in God for deliverance from a serious threat. Consider it joy to receive a test, having experienced the fact that passing these tests leads toward maturity.

> Romans 5:3, 4 – *And not only so, but we glory in tribulations also, knowing that tribulation worketh patience; And patience, experience; and experience, hope:*

> James 1:2-4 – *My brethren, count it all joy when ye fall into various trials, knowing this, that the testing of your faith worketh*

> *patience. But let patience have her perfect work, that ye may be perfect and entire, lacking nothing.*

It should be every believer's desire to progress to spiritual maturity as rapidly as possible. It is the author's *opinion* that the quickest one could obtain a thorough knowledge of the Word with a concentrated study would be about three years. This time period would naturally depend on God's providing appropriate trials and tests throughout that period.

The next chapter deals with what faces the believer who chooses to remain in spiritual immaturity.

[1] Greek, *aner teleios*, "mature man." The word *aner* is used to distinguish man from woman; and the word *teleios* means mature (ripe, fully aged, complete). Biblically, being mature means to have a thorough knowledge of the plan and will of God (cf. Romans 12:1, 2; Colossians 1:9-11; 4:12; II Timothy 3:17). (It *does not* indicate sinless perfection.) One can know the right thing to do and still choose not to do it.

Aner is used not to exclude a *gune*, Greek for "woman," from becoming mature in Biblical knowledge, but for several other reasons given below:

   a) The man is referred to since only he is to be the teacher (Ephesians 4:11; James 3:1).

   b) Women are not to teach men or to exercise authority over them (I Corinthians 14:34, 35; I Timothy 2:11-14).

   c) No matter how knowledgeable a woman becomes, she is still more subject to Satanic deception than is the man (I Timothy 2:14; II Timothy 3:6, 7).

d) The man came of age in Israel when he turned twenty years old. Then he was counted in the census, gave his own sacrifices, and could serve in the military. *Aner teleios* probably is used Biblically to stand for a twenty-year-old male ready to enter spiritual warfare and to be accountable for himself.

e) A mature man should also be ready to teach others (II Timothy 3:17; James 3:1, 2).

f) A woman can learn and understand doctrine as well as any man and thus become spiritually mature. (The man in "every man of" Colossians 1:28 means mankind generically.)

Psalm 30: 2, 3 *O Lord, my God, I cried unto thee, and thou hast healed me. O Lord, thou hast brought up my soul from sheol; thou hast kept me alive, that I should not go down to the pit.*

Psalm 116: 7-9 *Return unto thy rest, O my soul; for the Lord hath dealt bountifully with thee. For thou hast delivered my soul from death, mine eyes from tears, and my feet from falling. I will walk before the Lord in the land of the living.*

Chapter 12

DIVINE DISCIPLINE

God is extremely serious that *every* believer should become spiritually mature. Only mature believers have the ability to overcome the world's influences and their own flesh:

> II Corinthians 10:3-5 – *For though we walk in the flesh, we do not war after the flesh (For the weapons of our warfare are not carnal, but mighty through God to the pulling down of strongholds), Casting down imaginations, and every high thing that exalteth itself against the knowledge of God, and bringing into captivity every thought to the obedience of Christ;*

Additionally, since the entire Christian life is a supernatural way of life, it is difficult for spiritual babies to function effectively in any area. To function as a disciple to unbelievers (Matthew 28:19,20), to identify and utilize your spiritual gift to other believers (I Corinthians 12; I Peter 4:10), and even to function in your priesthood* (I Peter 2:5-9), are largely based on your knowledge of the Word – spiritual maturity.

And just what is the alternative to reaching spiritual maturity? What if a believer learns about the doctrine of eternal security and then simply drops out of the Christian life shortly after salvation, or turns his back on Christ at any time? We certainly would not want to be in his shoes. Pressure and trials will follow him throughout his life as God the Father will chastise His rebellious child. If a believer faces his trials with an attitude of disbelief, complaining, ignorance, or a hardened heart he will receive chastisement until he rectifies his condition and confesses his sin to God.

> Deuteronomy 8:5, 6 – *Thou shalt also consider in thine heart, that, as a man chasteneth his son, so the Lord thy God chasteneth thee. Therefore thou shalt keep the commandments of the Lord thy God, to walk in his ways, and to fear him.*
>
> Psalm 118: 17, 18 – *I shall not die, but live, and declare the works of the Lord. The Lord hath chastened me very much, but he hath not given me over unto death.*
>
> * The priesthood is the personal, private relationship with God consisting of: worship, confession, giving, prayer, praise, thanksgiving, communion, service to God.

> Proverbs 3:11, 12 – *My son, despise not the chastening of the Lord, neither be weary of his correction. For whom the Lord loveth he correcteth, even as a father the son in whom he delighteth.*
>
> I Corinthians 11:32 – *But when we are judged, we are chastened of the Lord, that we should not be condemned with the world.*
>
> Revelation 3:19 – *As many as I love, I rebuke and chasten; be zealous, therefore, and repent.* (See also Psalm 6:1; 38:1; 94:12; Jeremiah 31:18, 19; Hebrews 12:5-13.)

If the estranged believer ignores these warnings, the chastisement will eventually turn to punishment.

> I Corinthians 16:22 – *If any man love[1] not the Lord Jesus Christ, let him be Anathema Maranatha.*[2]

Most believers who are being punished will not acknowledge what is happening to them. They just blame God for their misfortune and adjust to the pain of broken marriages, delinquent children, unsatisfactory work experiences, financial difficulties, and physical or mental illness. They may even experience the worst curses of all – acquiring money, fame, or success *without* the capacity to handle them. Certainly they cannot experience the peace and rest of being in Christ which is available to them.

> Hebrews 3:12 – *Take heed, brethren, lest there be in any of you an evil heart of unbelief, in departing from the living God.*

> Hebrews 4:1 – *Let us, therefore, fear lest, a promise being left us of entering into his rest, any of you should seem to come short of it.*

If a believer continues in his state of unbelief and progresses in his sin, he eventually will receive the sin unto death.

> I John 5:16 – *If any man see his brother sin a sin which is not unto death, he shall ask, and he shall give him life for them that sin not unto death.* **There is a sin unto death**; *I do not say that he shall pray for it.* (Emphasis ours.) (See also Joshua 23:16.)

I Corinthians 10:6-10 gives an overview of how thousands of believers in the Exodus generation committed various sins that led to their awful and premature deaths. These events are recorded for our warning:

> I Corinthians 10:11 – *Now all these things happened unto them for examples, and they are written for our admonition, upon whom the ends of the ages are come.*

God warns the children of Israel that all of the Exodus generation will die in the desert because of their murmuring against Him (Numbers 14:29-35).

An earthquake swallowed those who were part of the Korah rebellion, and God sent fire to kill 250 more (Numbers 16:30-35).

The children of Israel murmured against Moses and Aaron, and God sent a plague that killed 14,700 (Numbers 16:47-49).

The people challenged God and Moses, and God sent poisonous snakes to kill many (Numbers 21:5-9).

Some of the people committed idolatry, and 24,000 more died by plague (Numbers 25:1-9).

God's warning was fulfilled – none of the Exodus generation were left (Numbers 26:64, 65).

God uses a graphic example to explain the purpose He has for all believers' lives after salvation. Hebrews 3:7-19 is too long to quote here. Please read it and then note the following points, relating this passage to your life.

Summary and Application

1. God desired to give Israel the promised land of milk and honey as its possession forever (Exodus 3:17). He even promised to help Israel clean out the land of giants and heathen (Deuteronomy 3:22).

2. Israel was an estimated two million strong as it came out of the Egyptian bondage –603,550 men twenty years old or older (Numbers 1:46). All of the adults were saved as evidenced by their observing the first Passover (Exodus 12:1-13).

3. God took His huge kindergarten class through the Red Sea, drowned the entire Egyptian army, and led His whiny charges into the wilderness (Exodus 14:11-14).

4. For the next forty years God led these ungrateful, always-complaining, children

around in circles while trying to teach them to trust in Him and His Word (Hebrews 3:9).

5. Throughout this period God had provided sweet water out of bitter (Exodus 15:22-25), quail at night and manna every morning (Exodus 16:13), and water out of a rock (Exodus 17:6). He had conquered the invading army of Amalek (Exodus 17:13) and had given them the Mosaic Covenant.

6. But, the children of Israel hardened their hearts against God (Hebrews 3:8).

7. Finally, the entire adult generation that had come out of Egypt (except for Joshua and Caleb) died in the wilderness (Hebrews 3:17-19).

How Does This Relate?

8. God had a purpose for the nation of Israel to learn and to live by The Law while wandering in the desert. This was to prepare them to enter the promised land, subdue the heathen therein, and to glorify God.

    Likewise, God has a purpose for every Christian to learn the Word of God and so to become spiritually mature, prepared to battle Satan.

9. God's Word was taught to the Israelites for forty years, while God gave the people many specific opportunities to trust in Him.

    Likewise, God will provide His Word for you and give you opportunities to discover His matchless character.

10. The Israelites had an evil heart of disbelief throughout the forty years, and therefore the 603,550 male Jews of twenty years old and above died the sin unto death (except Caleb and Joshua, Numbers 1:46; 26:65). We are not told how the balance of the people served their penalty. Probably most died a natural, although premature, death since the youngest would have been only sixty years old had they lived. The average life expectancy at this time was about 120 years. (See Psalm 55:23.)

> Hebrews 3:17 – *But with whom was he grieved forty years? Was it not with them that had sinned, whose carcasses fell in the wilderness?*

Likewise, the Christian who hardens his heart today against God's Word and refuses to believe in the promises or character of God can find himself facing this same fate.

> I Corinthians 11:30 – *For this cause many are weak and sickly among you, and many sleep.* (See also Psalm 118:18; I Corinthians 10:1-11; I Corinthians 11:27-32; I John 5:16.)

11. God told the children of Israel that entering into the land would be entering into His rest by faith (Hebrews 3:18, 19).

Likewise, sinful Christians today can enter into God's rest by turning their hearts back to God.

> I John 1:9 – *If we confess our sins, he is faithful and just to forgive us our sins, and to cleanse us from all unrighteousness.*

> Hebrews 4:9-11 – *There remaineth, therefore, a rest to the people of God. For he that is entered into his rest, he also hath ceased from his own works as God did from his. Let us labor, therefore, to enter into that rest, lest any man fall after the same example of unbelief.* (See also Psalm 38; John 14:27.)

The choice is yours. You can easily see that God is a lot more serious about our Christian life than He is about the Sunday-only nod which most people reluctantly give to Him.

> Psalm 119:75-77a – *I know, O Lord, that thy judgments are right, and that thou in faithfulness hast afflicted me. Let, I pray thee, thy merciful kindness be for my comfort, according to thy word unto thy servant. Let thy tender mercies come unto me, that I may live.*

The following chart attempts to depict the rebellious believer's Christian Walk:

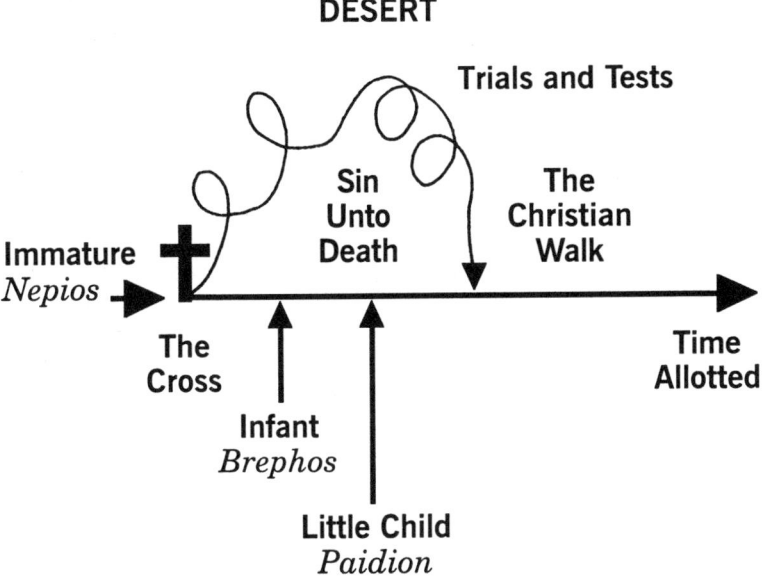

Chronological Development

This chart depicts a believer who remains spiritually immature and wanders in the place of testing – the desert. Without God's Word and power, he repeatedly fails the trials of the flesh (his own sin nature) and the tests of the world (false philosophies). Eventually, he dies the sin unto death after rejecting God's attempts to revive him.

The following Chart depicts the spiritual life of a beliver growing to maturity:

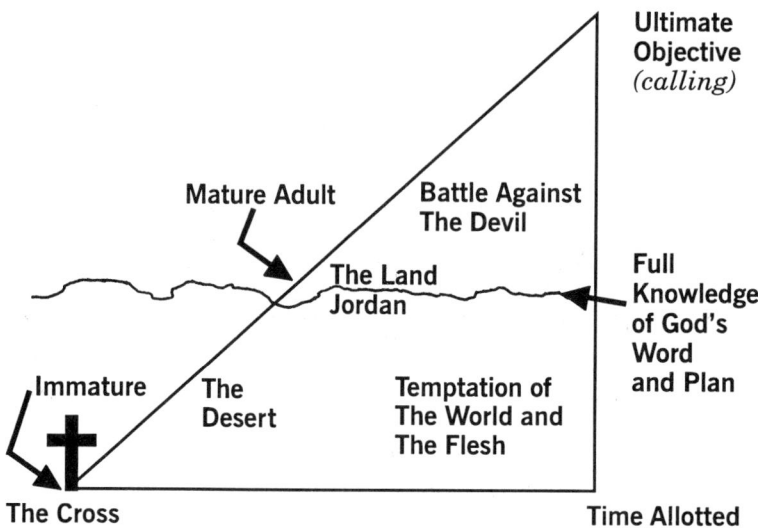

In the preceding chart the bottom line represents a person's time on Earth. The diagonal line represents the optimum path a believer could follow from salvation to maturity to fullfilling God's Purpose for his life. The lower section called, the desert, is the time of learning and testing. The upper section indicates a believer reaching maturity and crossing over the Jordan into the land fo milk and honey – and giants and Satan waring with God.

[1] Greek, *phileo*, "love," this word is used to express a love based on compatibility of intimate knowing, as between two brothers (John 15:14, 15).

[2] Greek, *Anathema Maranatha*, "literally one to be cursed by the Lord."

SECTION THREE

SUFFERING –
THE CHRISTIAN'S BADGE

Deuteronomy 29:29 The secret things belong unto the Lord our God; but those things which are revealed belong unto us and to our children forever, that we may do all the words of this law.

Acts 26:23 That Christ should suffer, and that he should be the first that should rise from the dead, and should show light unto the people, and to the Gentiles.

Chapter 13

CHRIST AND THE CHURCH

This chapter may well explain the most important concept about the Christian life. This concept is The Church[1] – the spiritual body of Christ, the invisible, universal representative of Christ on earth, the spiritual nation of priests, and the witness of the Gospel to all nations. The following are some aspects of The Church that Christians need to know:

- The Church was a mystery[2] in the Old Testament:

    Ephesians 3:2-6 – *If ye have heard of the dispensation of the grace of God which is given me toward you, How that by revelation he made known unto me the mystery (as I wrote before in few words,*

By which, when ye read, ye may understand my knowledge in the mystery of Christ) Which in other ages was not made known unto the sons of men, as it is now revealed unto his holy apostles and prophets by the Spirit. That the Gentiles should be fellow heirs, and of the same body, and partakers of his promise in Christ by the gospel. (See also Ephesians 5:32; Colossians 1:25-27.)

- Jesus Christ came to the nation of Israel to fulfill the Old Testament prophecies about the earthly reign by God (the Kingdom of Heaven or Kingdom of God) by the Seed of David (the Messiah):

Luke 1:31,32 – *And, behold, thou shalt conceive in thy womb, and bring forth a son, and shalt call his name Jesus. He shall be great, and shall be called the Son of the Highest; and the Lord God shall give unto him the throne of his father, David.* (See also II Samuel 7:16; Isaiah 9:6, 7; Luke 19:38; John 7:42; Romans 1:3.)

- Christ came to His own people, the Jews, but they rejected Him:

John 1:11 – *He came unto his own, and his own received him not.* (See also Matthew 4:17; 10:6; 15:24; Luke 17:25; Romans 15:8.)

- Therefore, Christ began to teach His disciples that Israel would be set aside while The Church would become the new chosen people of God:

Romans 11:25 – *For I would not, brethren, that ye should be ignorant of this mystery, lest ye should be wise in your own conceits: that blindness in part is happened to Israel, until the fullness of the Gentiles be come in.* (See also Matthew 13:10-15; 16:18, 21; 21:42, 43.)

- The Church came into existence on the day of Pentecost, exactly fifty days following the resurrection of the Lord Jesus Christ:

Acts 2:1-4 – *And when the day of Pentecost was fully come, they were all with one accord in one place. And suddenly there came a sound from heaven like a rushing mighty wind, and it filled all the house where they were sitting. And there appeared unto them cloven tongues as of fire, and it sat upon each of them, And they were all filled with the Holy Spirit, and began to speak with other tongues, as the Spirit gave them utterance.*

- The Church is the means for fulfilling God's historical plan for the salvation of the Gentile nations:

Romans 11:11 – *I say, then, Have they stumbled that they should fall? God forbid; but rather through their fall salvation is come unto the Gentiles, to provoke them to jealousy.* (See also Galatians 3:14; Ephesians 2:11-13; I Peter 2:9, 10.)

- Jesus Christ had to suffer and sacrifice His life to provide our salvation:

Philippians 2:8 – *And, being found in fashion as a man, he humbled himself and became obedient unto death, even the death of the cross.* (See also Titus 2:14; Hebrews 5:8; 10:10; I Peter 2:24; and many more.)

- At the point of salvation, every believer is spiritually baptized by the Holy Spirit into The Church:

I Corinthians 12:13 – *For by one Spirit were we all baptized into one body, whether we be Jews or Greeks, whether we be bond or free; and have been all made to drink into one Spirit.* (See also John 14:16, 17; Acts 1:5.)

- Christ is the spiritual head (leader, superior, chief) of The Church:

Colossians 1:18 – *And he is the head of the body, the church; who is the beginning, the firstborn from the dead, that in all things he might have the preeminence.* (See also Ephesians 1:22; 4:15; 5:23; Colossians 1:18; 2:10.)

- Christians make up the body (foot, hand, ear, eye, etc.) of the Church:

I Corinthians 12:27 – *Now ye are the body of Christ, and members in particular.* (See also I Corinthians 12:12-14; Romans 12:5; Ephesians 5:30.)

- Christ will return (Second Advent) after the fullness of the Gentiles comes, at which time The Church will be removed from Earth.

> Acts 1:11b – *This same Jesus, who is taken up from you into heaven, shall so come in like manner as ye have seen him go into heaven.* (See also Romans 11:25; I Thessalonians 4:14-17.)

It is beyond the scope of this book to resolve the many confusing problems concerning Covenant and Dispensational Theology. Appendix B attempts to overview Biblical Theology concerning Israel and the Church.

It is our identification with Christ and His Church that makes our lives so unique. It is important to realize that Christians are not Jews, and The Church is not Israel. The children of Israel were promised good health, financial prosperity, and safety from physical dangers – if they kept The Commandments of God. However, Christians have no such promise. Their promise is an earthly life of suffering, followed by an eternal life of glory and joy. Jesus Christ was an example to Christians as to how they could expect to suffer:

> I Peter 2:21 – *For even hereunto were ye called, because Christ also suffered for us, leaving us an example, that ye should follow his steps.*

After all, Christians are allowed to follow Christ in the first resurrection:

> I Corinthians 15:20 – *But now is Christ risen from the dead and become the firstfruits of them that slept.*

Colossians 1:18 – *And he is the head of the body, the church; who is the beginning, the firstborn from the dead, that in all things he might have the preeminence.* (See also Acts 26:23; I Corinthians 15:23.)

- Christ is the first fruits of all groups to be resurrected:

I Corinthians 15:23 – *But every man in his own order: Christ the first fruits; afterward they that are Christ's at his coming.*

The groups (order or troop) are:

1. Jesus Christ, the first-born.

2. All Christians from the beginning of the Church alive or asleep at Christ's second Advent (I Thessalonians 4:14-17).

3. The Old Testament saints plus those saints (martyrs) dying during the Tribulation (Isaiah 26:19; Daniel 12:2; Revelation 20:4).

These distinct groups (or orders) make up the first resurrection (Revelation 20:5,6). Finally, immediately after the millennium, is the second resurrection of all unbelievers to judgment and eternal death (Revelation 20:6, 13-15).

Why We Are Called Christians

- Christ is in The Church, all believers are in the Church.

- Christ suffered during His life on earth, all believers will suffer during their lives on earth.

- Christ was the first to be resurrected in His group, all believers will also be resurrected.//
- Christian's can be identified by their badge of suffering as Jesus suffered.

Christian Martyrs

Throughout the entire church age believers in one part of the world or another have been called on to suffer and die in the name of Christ. Foxe's book, *Christian Martyrs of the World* states that there were ten Roman persecutions beginning A.D. 64. The first was by Nero who had thousands of men and women killed, stripped naked and thrown into the streets. The Church grew. The second persecution began under Domitian who's hatred caused Christians to be disemboweled, torn apart, stoned, covered with hot plates of iron, strangled, eaten by wild animals, hung, and their bodies piled in a heap without burial. The Church grew. The third persection was under Emperor Trgian who was attributed to killing thousands of Christians *daily*. The Church continued to grow. By A.D. 249 the persecutions ceased, but the heathen temples of Rome were almost empty.

Of course persecution against The Church has continued under every totalarian government throughout history – from the Roman Catholic Church of the middle ages, to Nazi Germany, to Communist Russia, China, and many others. And, it will continue until Christ returns to rule.

[1] Greek, *ekklesia*, "the called out ones, assembly."

[2] Greek, *musterion*, "knowledge only known by an initiate of a secret order, *not* a mystery to an insider."

II Thessalonians 1:4 *So that we ourselves glory in you in the churches of God for your patience and faith in all your persecutions and tribulations that ye endure.*

Hebrews 2:9 *But we see Jesus, who was made a little lower than the angels for the suffering of death, crowned with glory and honor, that he, by the grace of God, should taste death for every man.*

Chapter 14

CHRIST'S SUFFERINGS ARE OUR EXAMPLE

Christ voluntarily gave up His rights and privileges as God and took on the inferior form of man:

> Philippians 2:5-7 – *Let this mind be in you, which was also in Christ Jesus, Who, being in the form of God, thought it not robbery to be equal with God, But made himself of no reputation, and took upon him the form of a servant, and was made in the likeness of men.* (See also II Corinthians 8:9; Hebrews 2:9, 16.)

This act of love on man's behalf was also an act of suffering personal loss. Christians may be called upon to give up any human positions of influence, wealth, or worldly respect in order to fulfill their role in God's Plan. (This is not to say one cannot have such positions, but that one should be able to give them up as did Christ.)

Jesus was tempted in His humanity in all ways as we are:

> Hebrews 4:15 – *For we have not an high priest who cannot be touched with the feeling of our infirmities, but was in all points tempted like as we are, yet without sin.* (See also Matthew 4:3-11.)

In the Matthew 4 passage cited above, Jesus is shown to be tempted while He was already suffering severe lack of food, water, and all other human comforts.

1. He was challenged by Satan to utilize His divine nature (which He had set aside when He became man) to make bread for His current fleshly need. To accept Satan's challenge would have disqualified Him from being the sacrifice for man's sins. Jesus passed the test!

2. Then Satan tempted Jesus to prove He was the Son of God (and that man really could live *by every word that proceeds out of the mouth of God*). He did this by tempting Jesus to call upon God to prove an Old Testament promise (Psalm 91:11, 12). Jesus did not need to prove that He was the Son of God or to challenge God to keep His Word. Jesus passed the test!

3. Satan offered Jesus the rulership of all the kingdoms of the world if He would prostrate Himself and worship him. This, of course, would have by-passed the suffering of the Cross and still resulted in rulership of a Kingdom. Jesus passed the test!

You have probably been tempted in some of these ways yourself:

- Have you ever been tempted to do something in your own power (such as talent or intelligence) where God would have you use His power instead? Example: Someone asks you for counsel because of your reputation for Biblical wisdom. You immediately shower the inquirer with a wealth of your opinions instead of first researching the Bible for God's advice.

- We have all wanted to call on God to prove His Word to us or others. The more beyond human understanding that we trust in God, the more we would like for Him to vindicate our position.

- Have you ever been tempted by the pleasures of the here and now to give up God's future promise? How often we are willing to settle for the crumbs of the immediate, which we can grab for ourselves, rather than wait for the unseen banquet God is preparing for those who trust in Him.

During the earthly ministry of Jesus, He suffered rejection even from His family and the disciples. His people, the Jews, the chosen ones of God, rejected His heritage, His person, and His message:

Luke 17:25 – *But first must he suffer many things, and be rejected of this generation.*

John 5:18 – *Therefore, the Jews sought the more to kill him, because he not only had broken the sabbath, but said also that God was his Father, making himself equal with God.* (See also Isaiah 53:3; Matthew 9:34; 13:15; 16:21; 23:37; Luke 17:25; 19:41, 42.)

Everyone has suffered rejection in his life but for you to feel the pain Christ must have felt, you would have to experience the personal rejection of your character, your love, or your sacrificial gift.

After the Lord's Supper Jesus, went to pray in the Garden of Gethsemane. Jesus knew that He would be put to death the next day. His human soul felt the suffering of emotional and mental anguish during this time when He anticipated the horrible torture of being separated from God while bearing all of the sins of the world – past, present, and future. This night would bring every form of nonphysical suffering to Jesus that a human being can experience:

- The Matthew 26:37-42 account describes Jesus as . . . *He began to be grieved* (to feel pain and sorrow) leading to depression (verse 37). He then told His disciples that His soul was *exceedingly sorrowful* (literally – surrounded with pain) even *unto death* (verse 38).

- The Mark 14:33-39 account describes Jesus to be . . . *sore amazed* (amazed, astonished, awestruck), again leading to depression

> (verse 33). He then told His disciples that His soul was *exceedingly sorrowful* (literally, surrounded with pain) even *unto death* (verse 34).
>
> In both of these accounts, Jesus also virtually begged God the Father to take away the cup He must drink – the sins of the world poured out on His perfect, sin-free soul (Matthew 26:39-44).
>
> - The Luke 22:42-44 account does not have any of the previously used emotional/mental pain words. Instead, it states that after Jesus began to pray He became involved in a violent struggle (with self or Satan?) and prayed so intensely that his sweat became as drops of blood (*diapedesia*, verse 44).

Most humans have not reached the depths of despair that Jesus reached in the garden. His emotional/mental anguish caused enough pain to His soul to desire death as an escape. He even prayed that God would release Him from the very purpose for which His humanity had been called.

> Hebrews 2:9 – *But we see Jesus, who was made a little lower than the angels **for the suffering of death**, crowned with glory and honor, that he, by the grace of God, **should taste death for every man**.* (Emphasis ours.)

Even when a person arrives at this point of despair, it is usually due to something he caused himself. Whether your pain or depression comes from sin, failure, or legitimate sorrow for yourself, God has a solution. Set your eyes on the big picture – God has a plan for your life, which at the moment may be miserable. Confess your sins (including any self pity), pray for guidance, and expect an answer. God would love to comfort and strengthen you.

The next morning Jesus suffered betrayal from Judas, false testimony against Him in court, and illegal judicial processes leading to an unfair and immoral judgment. No sin was ever found in Him (II Corinthians 5:21; I Peter 2:21).

After the unjust verdict, Jesus was led to His death sentence surrounded by a vicious pack of sinners who spat on Him, slapped Him with the palms of their hands, whipped Him about His head and face, jammed a wreath of thorns down on His head, and ridiculed Him all the way to the cross. By the time He reached the cross, the face of Jesus was so disfigured that He could not be recognized as Jesus, *or even as a man* (Isaiah 52:14). Finally, He was nailed to the cross and lifted up. Psalm 22 describes the ways Jesus experienced the torture of the cross:

- *I am poured out like water,*
- *all my bones are out of joint:*
- *my heart is like wax; it is melted within me.*
- *My strength is dried up.*
- *my tongue cleaveth to my jaws;*
- *For dogs have compassed me;*
- *the wicked have enclosed me;*
- *they pierced my hands and my feet;*
- *I may count all of my bones;*
- *they look and stare upon me.*

Jesus was crucified at 9 A.M. and hung on the cross suspended by only three nails while He was on display. At 12 P.M. it became dark as night for a period of three hours while Jesus bore the sins of every man, woman, and child in the world – past, present, and future. He suffered spiritual death during this final phase as He was separated from God the Father and God the Holy Spirit. About 3 P.M., Jesus cried aloud, *"My God, My God, Why hast thou forsaken me?"* He cried out again loudly, but not discernibly, then *yielded up the spirit*, laying down His physical life (Matthew 27:50). The gospel of John reports that just prior to dismissing His own Spirit, Jesus also said, *"It is finished."* The perfect sacrifice for mankind's sin had been completed:

> Hebrews 10:12 – *But this man, after he had offered one sacrifice for sins forever, sat down on the right hand of God.*

The physical body of Jesus was buried and was resurrected after three days. He ministered to the disciples on earth for forty days, and then ascended to the throne of God, where He was accepted and glorified as the first human being to enter into heaven. Since this greatest of sacrifices, Christians have been called to endure suffering as a testimony to Jesus Christ until His return at the Second Advent.

Christ's Story

No one's story could match the reality of Christ's life. He set aside His position of honor, power, and glory to become the form of a man. He was rejected by those He came to serve and to lead. He was defiled by every form of injustice known to man. I do not believe anything we could suffer would match the suffering of Jesus Christ. Perhaps when we give up our "rights" and suffer on behalf of another we might feel a little of His pain. Such as when a great athlete gives up a professional career because he knows God would have him prepare for and serve as a missionary; or when an intelligent, creative, young woman chooses to submit her life Biblically to her husband; or when a highly trained businessman happily agrees to serve as deacon of church maintenance in all humility. *Maybe we can experience a very small amount of the loss and humiliation that Christ experienced.*

Colossians 2:6, 7 *As ye have, therefore, received Christ Jesus the Lord, so walk ye in him, Rooted and built up in him, and established in the faith, as ye have been taught, abounding therein with thanksgiving.*

Philippians 1:29 *For unto you it is given in the behalf of Christ, not only to believe on him but also to suffer for his sake.*

Chapter 15

THE CHRISTIAN WALK

The Christian Walk is when a believer actually lives out his spiritual maturity on a day-by-day basis. It is accomplished when a believer imitates Christ's character in each life situation. Paul commanded the believers at Corinth to become imitators of him as he was of Christ.

> 1 Corinthians 11:1 – *Be ye followers of me, even as I also am of Christ.* (See also Philippians 3:17.)

> I John 2:6 – *He that saith he abideth in him ought himself also so to walk, even as he walked.*

The Christian who consistently submits his will to God, who practices being filled with the Holy Spirit by confessing all known sins to God, and who commits himself to becoming spiritually mature by mastering the Word of God should begin to take on the image of Christ:

II Corinthians 3:18 – *But we all, with unveiled face beholding as in a mirror the glory of the Lord, are changed into the same image from glory to glory, even as by the Spirit of the Lord.* (See also Romans 8:29.)

Thus, the Christian's life (walk) will become more and more Christlike:

1. **in love** . . . Ephesians 5:2a *And walk in love, as Christ also hath loved us.* (See also II John 1:6.)

2. **worthily and in good works** . . . Colossians 1:10 *That ye might walk worthy of the Lord unto all pleasing, being fruitful in every good work, and increasing in the knowledge of God.* (See also Ephesians 2:10; 4:1; I Thessalonians 2:12; 4:1.)

3. **in the Holy Spirit** . . . Galatians 5:25 *If we live in the Spirit, let us also walk in the Spirit.* (See also Romans 8:4; Galatians 5:16; Ephesians 5:8; I John 1:7.)

4. **in wisdom and honesty before unbelievers** . . . I Thessalonians 4:12 *That ye may walk honestly toward them that are outside, and that ye may have lack of nothing.* (See also Romans 13:13; Colossians 4:5.)

5. **NOT in the carnal flesh like unbelievers** . . . II Peter 2:10 *But chiefly them that walk after the flesh in the lust of uncleanness, and despise government. Presumptuous are they, selfwilled, they are not afraid to speak evil of dignities.* (See also I Corinthians 3:3;

Ephesians 4:17; II Thessalonians 3:11; Jude 1:18.)

It is clearly God's purpose for every believer to live so that his or her life represents Christ, and not the world. But remember, the spiritual life can only be lived *in the Spirit*, not by human effort. Christianity is the way you live your life, not the bumper sticker your car wears.

Suffering as a Christian

An integral part of the Christian Walk is suffering on behalf of Christ. Every believer who lets his faith be known will suffer just because he is a Christian. Examples are: the man who is ridiculed for giving an honest day's work for his pay; or the employee who refuses to drink with management for a promotion; or the wife who sticks by a difficult marriage while she is being encouraged by others to take the easy way out. Naturally, any such suffering must be for righteousness sake to be bonafide "for Christ." I once knew a young believer who was extremely proud that he had been fired from his job because he had been witnessing to others while he was being paid to work. Had he been fired for witnessing on his own time it might have been persecution; however, being fired for stealing (not doing what he was paid to do) is not suffering on Christ's behalf.

Each Christian faces differing degrees of suffering – it could be little, like rejection from one you do not respect anyway; it could be terminal cancer for the thirty-year-old mother of four, or it could be a husband and father deserted by his childhood bride for another man. It is really all the same. Suffering is any tribulation, pain, injury, injustice, illness, hardship, pressure, tragedy, heartache, or depravation *that God allows into your life*. Christianity that is sold as being "happy, happy, happy," as some superficial modern songs portray, is Biblically incorrect. Suffering is normal to the Christian Walk:

> Philippians 1:29 – *For unto you it is given in the behalf of Christ, not only to believe on him but also to suffer for his sake.*

> I Peter 2:21 – *For even hereunto were ye called, because Christ also suffered for us, leaving us an example, that ye should follow his steps;*

> I Peter 4:12 – *Beloved, think it not strange concerning the fiery trial which is to test you, as though some strange thing happened unto you.*

All this discussion about suffering reminds me of an old Country and Western song from *many* years ago. It began:

> ***Gloom, despair and agony on me.***
> ***Deep dark depression, excessive misery.***
> ***If it weren't for bad luck***
> ***I'd have no luck at all –***
> ***Gloom, despair and agony on me!***

> Credit: Roy L. Clark, *Hee Haw*, July 13, 1999

Sometimes the suffering part of the Christian Life can seem as depressing as this song. When our Lord Jesus was facing His most painful suffering in the Garden, we have seen that He certainly felt this despondent and depressed. When He looked over Jerusalem knowing its people would reject Him and that their souls would be lost as a result, He wept. Obviously, Psalm 32:3, 4 and Psalm 51 portray David in the agony of suffering divine discipline. Many other examples, such as Psalm 77 and the book of Job, should help you to forgive yourself if you have ever felt depressed under the weight of suffering, whatever its reason. As it was for these believers, God's strength is sufficient for you, too!

Perhaps the following verses will help believers grasp the benefits that God has in mind for them as a result of their sufferings:

> John 12:26 – *If any man serve me, let him follow me; and where I am, there shall also my servant be: if any man serve me, him will my Father honor.*
>
> Romans 8:17 – *And if children, then heirs – heirs of God, and joint-heirs with Christ – if so be that we suffer with him, that we may be also glorified together.*
>
> II Corinthians 4:17 – *For our light affliction, which is but for a moment, worketh for us a far more exceeding and eternal weight of glory.*
>
> II Timothy 2:12a – *If we suffer, we shall also reign with him.*
>
> I Peter 4:13 – *But rejoice, inasmuch as ye are partakers of Christ's sufferings, that, when his glory shall be revealed, ye may be glad also with exceeding joy.*

Specifically, a believer's minor suffering on behalf of Christ, His Word, or even right living will result in his glorification and joy in eternity. If Christians are allowed the opportunity to suffer for the sake of Christ, they should thank God for the privilege:

James 1:2 – *My brethren, count it all joy when ye fall into various trials.*

I Peter 4:16 – *Yet, if any man suffer as a Christian, let him not be ashamed, but let him glorify God on this behalf.*

I Peter 4:19 – *Wherefore, let them that suffer according to the will of God commit the keeping of their souls to him in well-doing, as unto a faithful Creator.*

Suffering Always Has a Purpose

Suffering in one person's life is often intended by God to benefit others as well. For the recipient, it might be to glorify God, while it might be discipline for another (like a husband or wife), for others it could be testing of their dependence on God, and in others it could be an opportunity for sharing or praying for the one in need.

Of course, suffering for the rebellious believer is intended by God to bring a change of attitude (repentance) toward Him. Rebellion is the knowing and willing rejection of God's standards (Hebrews 12:5-13). Suffering for disobedience is the consequence for non-defiant breaking of standards which are known or the lack of interest in learning God's Word (Hebrews 5:11, 12). In these cases, suffering is meant to press the immature believer toward Christian maturity so that he can better represent Christ on earth.

Suffering of the believer growing toward maturity is to provide the tests necessary for him to learn dependence on God – i.e., His Character, His Word, and His Power (Romans 5:3-5; James 1:2-4). In this case, God's objective is to give the believer a test He knows that he can pass. (God's Word uses the Greek word *dokimos* in

James 1:3, translated *trying,* and twice in Romans 5:4, translated *experience,* to describe this test. *Dokimos* means "to approve after testing; proved, tried, accepted, examined.") Every immature believer needs tests (trials) at various stages of his spiritual growth in order to experience both progress and deficiencies. Every test passed causes the believer to move one step closer to reaching God's calling for his life:

> Phillippians 3:12 – *Not as though I had already attained, either were already perfect; but I follow after, if that I may apprehend that for which also I am apprehended of Christ Jesus.*

> Phillippians 3:14 – *I press toward the mark for the prize of the high calling of God in Christ Jesus.*

Finally, suffering of the mature believer glorifies God, instructs the angels, embarrasses Satan, and is a testimony to God. Abel, Enoch, Noah, Sarah, Abraham, Isaac, Jacob, Joseph, Moses, Rahab, Gideon, Barak, Samson, Jephthae, David, Samuel; and the prophets are examples as confirmed in Hebrews 11:11-32. Obviously, Job (probably Shadrach, Meshach, and Abednego as well), Paul, Stephen, Timothy, Titus, and the other apostles were also mature believers who suffered for God.

> **NOTE:** None of these believers were perfect in their walk. They all failed – some rarely like Joseph; others more often, like Abraham, David, and Peter. But, they all passed most of the tests God gave them. God never keeps track of a Christian's failures. He only charts their progress, the intent of their heart, and whether they ultimately reach His objectives. This is an example of the matchless grace of God.

The Christian Walk

Thousands of men and women have attempted to live the Christian Walk. Most of these dedicated Christians are average people like you and me. I think that I have known some of them in my lifetime – a teacher here, an aunt there, and perhaps even a pastor. No one has written about the majority of these people, and any knowledge of their walk with God is unknown or forgotten by man after a generation or two, but certainly never forgotten by God. The following are some comments about one such man's walk with God:

A. W. TOZER

"A. W. Tozer's conversion to Christianity came when he was seventeen. As a result he gained an insatiable hunger and thirst for the things of God. A cleaned-out area in the family's basement became his refuge where he could pray and meditate on the goodness of God.

"Shortly after their marriage the Tozers made a pact to trust God for all their needs regardless of the circumstances. Tozer never swayed from this principle. Material things were never an issue. Many have said if Tozer had food, clothing, and his books, he was content. The family never owned a car. Tozer, instead, opted for the bus and train for travel. Even after becoming a well-known Christian author, Tozer signed away much of his royalties to those who were in need. His message was as fresh as it was uncompromising. His single purpose in life was to know God personally, and he encouraged others to do the same. He quickly discovered that a deep, abiding relationship with God was something that had to be cultivated.

"During his lifetime, Tozer pastored several Christian and Missionary Alliance (CMA) churches, authored more than forty books, and served as editor of *Alliance Life*, the monthly denominational publication for CMA. At least two of Tozer's books are considered spiritual classics, *The Pursuit of God* and *The Knowledge Of The Holy* – a tremendous accomplishment for a man who never received a formal theological education. 'Tozer's sermons were never shallow,' writes Snyder. 'There was hard thinking behind them, and (he) forced his hearers to think with him. He had the ability to make his listeners face themselves in the light of what God was saying to them. The flippant did not like Tozer; the serious who wanted to know what God was saying to them loved him.'

"Leonard Ravenhill once said of Tozer, 'I fear that we shall never see another Tozer. Men like him are not college bred but Spirit taught. The wondrous pursuit of God is more than a legacy. It is a way of life passed on to us that we too might experience what A. W. Tozer lived. Have you begun your pursuit of God?"

© In Touch Ministries® ITM, Inc.

Summary

- The Christian Walk is accomplished when a believer lives out his spiritual maturity on a day-by-day basis. Such a believer will be imitating the character of Christ with his life.

- Suffering on behalf of Christ is a natural result of living for Christ.

- There are different types of suffering, but they are really all for the same purposes. It is the way the believer *handles* the suffering that brings glory to God. Such suffering is a testimony to unbelievers and an encouragement to other believers.

- Suffering can be a depressing intervention in our lives or a blessed opportunity. For it to be a blessing, we need to understand the benefits God has designed in eternity for those who persevere in this life.

- Suffering can be for approving, disciplining, promoting dependence on God, encouraging growth, or giving an opportunity for spiritual gifts to be used.

The next chapter will address the differing intensities of suffering between normal Christianity, historical periods of persecution of The Church, and leadership positions calling for all-out commitment.

*Onward, Christian soldiers,
Marching as to war,
With the cross of Jesus,
going on before.* *

Ephesians 6:11 *Put on the whole armor of God, that ye may be able to stand against the wiles of the devil.*

Chapter 16

THE CHRISTIAN SOLDIER

God calls a certain number of believers to serve Him in leadership roles. For example: Old Testament Patriarchs (Abraham, Isaac, Jacob, and Moses), Israel's Kings (all), High Priests (Aaron), Israel's Prophets (all), the eleven Apostles, and Paul. Examples of God's call to some of these leaders: Jacob (Isaiah 41:8), David (I Kings 11:34), Solomon (I Chronicles 28:5), the original twelve disciples/apostles (Matthew 10:2; John 6:70; 15:16; Acts 1:2), Paul (Acts 9:15); and even Jesus (Isaiah 42:1; Matthew 12:18; I Peter 2:4).

Christ specifically gave spiritual gifts of leadership to men in the early Church – the twelve apostles, prophets, evangelists, and pastor-teachers (elders, overseers, Ephesians 4:8, 11). Leaders are not the only soldiers in God's Army. God has an ultimate purpose *for each believer*. It is an individual's calling. That calling could

* Words copyrighted by J. Curwen & Sons, Ltd.

be as a missionary, deacon, church administrator, or any one of many service functions. However, it could just as easily be a doctor, business person, nurse, trucker, janitor, homemaker, government employee, or whatever. Only an individual will know how he is to serve God. He may get an idea of what his calling will be early in his Christian experience, but it will become more clear as he approaches maturity. God often calls us to spiritual tasks in areas where we were not previously proficient. Spiritual gifts, spiritual calling, and spiritual power mean that which *exceeds natural abilities*. If one demands to serve God with his own abilities, it will probably produce only works of the flesh (like Ishmael, Galatians 4:22, 23). Of course, God can add His supernatural power to one's natural talent; for example the rock singer who forsakes that type of music to glorify God with her beautiful voice.

Different Calls, Different Sufferings

Your calling may, or may not, relate directly to the suffering you will experience as a Christian. Naturally, those who serve on the front lines (pastors, public speakers, missionaries, and those in position of leadership) pay the highest cost. They are not only "shot" from the front by the enemy, but often from behind by fellow Christians.

Then there are the soldiers in the pew who lead fairly normal lives. They experience suffering for their own spiritual growth, to glorify God, as a testimony for Jesus Christ, as examples for other believers, as chastisement for rebellion, for proof of their faith, etc. Normally, they do not get on the front lines. However, there have been numerous times in history when all Christians – from Generals to foot soldiers, from cooks to mash personnel – are given the opportunity to represent Christ when the Church is being persecuted. Ten general persecutions by the Roman Empire against anyone who professed Christ as their Savior are recorded beginning about 67 A.D. and ending about 313 A.D. Hitler's vicious attack was not limited to only Jews; he also persecuted true Christians. Communism has also murdered millions of Christians over the past fifty years. Totalitarian governments must always eliminate those who are willing to die for their beliefs. But, consider this: suffering for one's beliefs, especially dying for them, is the strongest testimony to others of the truth of those beliefs.

Commitment

At some point after salvation, God calls every believer to service:

> I Corinthians 7:20 – *Let every man* (literally, each one) *abide in the same calling wherein he was called.*

> Ephesians 4:1 – *I therefore, the prisoner of the Lord, beseech you that ye walk worthy of the vocation to which ye are called,*

> I Peter 2:21 – *For even hereunto were ye called, because Christ also suffered for us, leaving us an example, that ye should follow his steps.*

I particularly enjoy God's use of average people who are committed to Him. A pastor once said,

> "Instead of being a large earthen crock, one may turn out to be just a tiny, fragile vessel. There are those who had hoped to be strong and healthy, and actively participate in God's service, but have become frail and delicate; yet they speak with rejoicing of the Lord's constant and sustaining love.

I knew a mother whose body was racked with pain and weakness all the years of her marriage; yet suffering ones came from far and near to hear from her lips what it means that *God's grace is sufficient.* There is another, a chronic invalid, who from her bed of illness sends messages of comfort and cheer to thousands of troubled souls throughout the world. She did not become what she once had hoped to be, but God made of her *another vessel* as it seemed good to Him."

A Christian's acknowledgment of God's call on his life is usually made in stages:

> Matthew 16:24 – *Then said Jesus unto his disciples, If any man will come after me, let him deny himself, and take up his cross, and follow me.*

- **First stage** – He must have the continuing desire to follow Christ. This indicates internal heart (mentality) motivation and a conscious decision of will, not an emotional response. Peter responded emotionally to Christ in John 13:37. Talk is cheap. Following Christ is a day-by-day decision.

- **Second Stage** – He must deny himself (Romans 6:12, 13; 12:1; Galatians 5:24). This means not only to separate from sin, but also to give up on all previous desires –even if acceptable – which interfere with following Christ. (II Timothy 2:4).

- **Third Stage** – Take up his cross. To be willing to suffer any pressure and even death that his calling may bring.

- **Fourth Stage** – Follow Christ. He continues following Christ's will for his life. Abraham followed God's call even when he didn't know where he was to go (Hebrews 11:8).

While salvation is a one-time decision, . . . *Believe on the Lord Jesus Christ and thou shalt be saved* . . . (Acts 16:31b), the decision to respond to God's call on a believer's life is not. Following Christ is a step-by-step, moment-by-moment decision to deny self and all personal *rights*, to carry whatever burden is allotted in a God honoring manner (no whining), and to trust God enough to follow Christ even in total darkness.

Unfortunately, few Christian leaders today are *sold out* (sometimes called the Exchanged Life, the Highest Life, the Powerful Life, the Prevailing Life, the Dynamic Life, the Victorious Life by well-known believers in the past). Obviously then, even fewer Christian non-leaders are being taught and encouraged to make such a commitment. (A pastor of one of America's largest churches once said he could count less than ten *sold out* Christians in his twenty-five-year ministry.)

Let us see how God's call and a believer's answer works out in actual experience:

JOURNEY OF A CHRISTIAN SOLDIER

"When I first became a believer at twenty seven years old, I was ready (like Peter) to die for Christ. I was eager to learn about God and His Plan and to become a soldier against Satan. The first part of my life I had dedicated to me. I had tried for success and personal fulfillment my own way and failed. Now, I was ready to serve the One who had bought me – my Lord. Within a week of my salvation I told my wife that I felt God was going to use me as an evangelist (a big, important one, of course – I still had my pride).

"For the next six years I intensely studied the Word and while at a Bible conference in 1971 told my wife I had made a decision that would affect the rest of our lives. I said, we need to give up all claims to physical wealth or things and get into a position to serve God wherever He chooses [desire to serve]. Being a godly woman, she reconfirmed my calling. Within six months we discovered God's first assignment of many to come:

1. "My wife and I sold our first home (in Dallas, Texas), stored our furniture, bought a travel trailer for our family of five to travel and live in, and headed off to find a homestead in Colorado and to begin home schooling our children [deny self]. A few months later we were able to sell the trailer because God had provided a cabin on a beautiful piece of property in the Colorado mountains.

    "Our resolve to give up everything and follow wherever God would lead was soon tested. We faced blizzards, no water and/or electricity, isolation from society, and the worst suffering of all – jealousy from some of the families who had invested with us in the property that we had found. This was the first time we had faced attacks from Christian friends and it was very painful to bear [take up our cross]. We left Colorado a year later with nothing for our investment. However, what God had given to us that year was far beyond the cost we had paid of ourselves or financially. We had grown much closer as a family. All three of our children had learned much about a God who had become real to them. Their study, work, and service habits had greatly improved. They had become much more responsible for their actions than most children ever do.

"My wife and I learned that while you can not always count on man (even other Christians), you can always count on God. We also learned that God always has a next step mapped out in His plan, even if it takes a different direction from where you thought you were going [follow Christ].

You can see repeated acts of self denial, taking up the cross, and following Christ in the next four calls. This is not meant to give us any credit, *For it is God which worketh in you both to will and to do of his good pleasure* (Philippians 2:13).

2. "God provided our next assignment through a Christian man, who was also involved in our Colorado venture. This man saw our family's total commitment to serve God and offered me the position of Business Manager of his new company. I had no education or experience in business, but God was about to train me. Again trusting in God wholly our family moved back to Dallas, Texas; and I took charge of the finances, production, order processing, and general management of a fast-growing company. God built that company (Accelerated Christian Education) from one million dollars in revenue to over four million within the next three years (1973-1976). Many sixty-and seventy-hour weeks were needed to handle this

company's rapid growth with my lack of experience. Eventually, I realized that my ministry at A.C.E. was over in July 1975 and gave them a one-year notice. A few weeks later, the board of directors offered me a huge pay raise and a completely paid-for masters' degree. Even though I had no idea where God wanted me next, I knew that I was not to stay with A.C.E. I received a nice bonus for my contribution and God blessed us in many other ways for our service.

3. "My wife and I started a Christian school. I started to teach a regular Bible class, investigated the prospects for establishing a new seminary, and researched child training from only the Bible. We eventually moved to Austin, Texas, in 1978 to share the teaching in a friend's church and to continue Biblical research. Over the next few years I established the Foundation for Biblical Research, and wrote the book, *What the Bible Says About . . . Child Training*. After presenting a child training seminar in over sixty churches and video taping a master, I determined my ministry was over in Austin. By September, 1981, the pastor I had come to help quit his ministry; the funding I had raised for the Foundation was drying up; and a woman was being used by Satan to try to destroy my family and our life's ministry. (Note: Neither Satan nor his demons are responsible for everything negative that happens to a believer; however, the more one learns and serves, the easier it is to spot Satan's tactic of deception.)

4. "I soon received a call from the Chairman of Alpha Omega Publication's Board of Directors, asking if I would be interested in and available to become President of that company. I evaluated the company's condition and easily realized that it was in very bad shape. It had $2.1 million in losses and no operating capital; $240,000 in delinquent bills; a $300,000 defaulted bank note, $250,000 in past due receivables, four lawsuits pending against it; IRS and SEC investigations threatening; and employee morale problems. God alone would receive the glory if this Christian company could be pulled out of the pit. I was voted in as the new Chairman of the Board and Chief Executive Officer by a vote of four to three. This authority was needed to turn the company around quickly. I later gave up the Chairmanship position voluntarily.

"The next twelve years were challenging, rewarding, and painful. The company became a model business by treating all vendors, creditors, customers, and employees honestly and fairly. The company assets grew slowly to $2.4 million with $6 million in annual revenue my last year (6/30/94). I spoke at about forty state home school conventions, wrote two books on home schooling, and set the direction for A.O.P. each year. My wife and I firmly believed we were where God wanted us. Nevertheless, the forces of evil continued their campaign to neutralize or even destroy this battle-weary solider. For various reasons one of the board members had to be removed from the board and even though he had nothing against me prior to his removal, he then blamed me for all his troubles. He wrote poison pen letters and sent them *everywhere*, claiming I was everything from Hitler to Jim Jones, a thief to a psychological misfit, a womanizer to a professional gambler, and guilty of fraud to embezzling. His attack to remove me as C.E.O. of the company, to discredit me among the nation's home schoolers, and to destroy my name and books went on for seven long years. This, even though our board of directors (seven honest, responsible, Christian business men) checked out and cleared me from every charge he made over the years.

"I learned to conduct business while someone was trying to destroy me with slander. I only stayed at A.O.P. to prove the charges wrong, to protect the investment of the shareholders, and to protect the employee's jobs. I learned that a fight could be fought by only one combatant and that it does not require two enemies to have a dispute. The most painful thing of all was seeing people who had known me for years listen to unsubstantiated claims and obviously hysterical attacks and still wonder, *if there is smoke there must be fire*.

"And the attacks continued. Finally, an outsider raided the company's stockholders and with threatened lawsuits and intimidation against the board members (who were weary of the fight as well), took over the company in November, 1994. Most of my managers, myself, and all who were loyal to me were fired. This was a shock, but only one of many to come. I not only lost my ministry, my career, and my income, but we also lost an excellent health insurance plan and $285,000 of our retirement plan. At fifty-five and having been under terrible stress for the past fifteen years, I did not have the drive to start over. But glory be to God. I learned not to return evil for evil and that the battle truly is the Lord's. I had come to love my wife more during this period of life than ever before. I also learned to care for others and even to pray for my enemies.

5. "I was not interested in going back into business again, but I could still perform Biblical research, write, and lecture on God's Word. So we decided to travel. (Of course, we knew I could find a *normal* job and avoid much of the suffering we might now face; but preaching the Word was our lifes' purpose.) Again, we sold our home (number four), stored our furniture, and bought a travel trailer. We hired another displaced manager to set up seminars for us to speak. By September, 1995, we were on the road lecturing at about three churches per week.

"And, now the real suffering began. Just turning around another Christian business near bankruptcy, becoming the first major Christian publisher to support home school parents, writing and lecturing nationwide to give encouragement to those considering home schooling had only earned me the rantings of one demoniac-acting agent (at one point my self-appointed enemy even ridiculed the Bible as being a source of viable information for child training). Satan now made it perfectly clear that this new ministry would cost us dearly. (We already had an idea because of the pressure surrounding the child training book and seminars, plus the tremendous suffering Virginia bore with the writing of her book, *On the Other Side of the Garden*.) This is because it is well known that Satan wants to destroy the family, the authority of the man, the submissive attitude of the woman, and Biblical child training. The following is a simplified listing of the pressures that just "happened" in the next five years.

* "After missing two quarterly payments (1/15 and 4/15/95) of my and my wife's royalties, I learned that the new owners of A.O.P. were contesting the payment of my royalties which had been approved and authorized by A.O.P.'s Board of Directors and paid for the past *eleven years*. This act cost us about $8,000 in income per year when it was most needed.

* "About one month into our speaking tour (10/95) Hurricane Opal began to chase us in Mississippi across Florida's panhandle, hitting Pensacola about the time we set up in Gainesville. It flew almost directly over us into Georgia as our travel trailer rocked back and forth.

* "My wife, who was already afflicted with a connective tissue disease and Trigeminal Neuralgia, suffered increased pain on the road. Mold spores, the bouncing of the truck, and talking a lot all hurt her. Two ruptured discs in my lower back hurt more as we traveled as well.

* "I developed severe pain in my upper back. This caused me to cancel two seminars and to lay over in Dallas while I went to a doctor. He diagnosed Spondolytis after taking x-rays and said no traveling or picking up boxes.

* "I finally had to tell our seminar director that his last date in April would have to be our final, and God graciously held us together for the last four months of our tour. I was also able to speak at two state home school conventions in May, 1996.

* "If it hadn't been for our severe physical suffering, we would probably still be on the road, ministering to people face to face.

"By April, 1996, we were back in Phoenix, bought a used mobile home in a retirement park, sold the travel trailer, and retrieved our belongings from storage. It was obvious that A.O.P. had no intention of paying royalties on my three books, video and audio series, and study guide. We could have sued them, but the cost would be more than we could afford. Therefore, I decided to write and print second editions for my books and to master a new video and audio seminar. By Christmas, 1996, the new editions had replaced the old at the major book distributors and both tapes and books were selling on our newly designed Internet bookstore. Needless to say, A.O.P. soon stopped selling their out-of-date editions. However, my back royalties have still not been paid at this point.

"Since then my wife and I have been operating our bookstore. She plans to write a sequel to her book, while I have been planning several books on *Suffering*, *Biblical Manhood*, *The Five Facets of the Believer*, and *Resolving the Arminianism/Calvinism Arguments*. Has the attack stopped now that we are not on the road? You judge:

* "We discovered I had developed Type II diabetes (9/96).

* "Virginia has had several serious bouts with her TN, severe shocks through her facial nerves and teeth. The only relief for her is to be numbed with Tegratol and endure its side effects of dizziness, exhaustion, and loss of concentration.

* "The difficulties of running a business out of a small home with just two people are legend (lots) and exhausting for two ill soldiers. Our bedroom is also the accounts payable and receivable departments, plus the order filing and shipping department. Our inventory lives behind our chairs in the living and dining room, and the second bedroom is my research and writing office.

* "The publisher of the second edition of *What the Bible Says About . . . Child Training* has had difficulty keeping it in print. We have lost about nine months of income because of this and have received hundreds of calls from individuals and book stores wanting copies.

* "I developed shingles in July, 1998, and at the same time developed an extremely painful catch in my neck muscles. I thought it was a neuropathy brought on by shingles. Whatever it is, we have spent over $3000 trying to stop the pain, on chiropractors, nerve blocks, vitamins, and medication, without success. So, I write every day through a wall of pain with the frequent use of ice packs and rest breaks.

* These are not all of the pressures we faced druing this period; some of the more incidental ones were: two root canals with after pain of almost a year each, three other caps, the printing press that broke only doing our run, the cover that ruined another run, the girl that drove her midget car under my back bumper and totalled her car, the hot water tank that broke, the evaporative cooler that needed repair, overnight mail to and from our editor taking weeks, and whatever.

"Yes, I think Satan is alive and active on planet Earth. As long as we continue to serve God and act as soldiers against Satan, his dominion, and his worldly philosophies, we will be subject to attack. Serving God is not a romantic dream. It is a real commitment to enlist in God's army against a terrifying foe. But we know that *Greater is He that is in you, than he that is in the world* (I John 4:4b). Suffering is a small price to pay to experience the power and provision of God in our life.

"And, how about the Lord's provision for us during the past five years? It has more than offset the pain. We love having the opportunity to work together, to receive the letters and phone calls from people God has helped through our materials. Every week one or two will call saying how Ginny's book saved their marriage, or how my book helped them turn around a child going in the wrong direction. Praise God that He allows us to see some of the fruit of our ministry. We have heard of men, women, and children being saved through our material. What greater joy could we have for laying down our lives? We have even had several families help in our financial support during these five years. We have been able to thank God for motivating these servants. Praise God for their faithfulness!"

J. Richard and Virginia Fugate

Answering God's Call For Leadership

Is this really necessary? Being trained for spiritual warfare and spiritual service seems like a lot on top of providing a living, raising a family, and having a little personal recreation. Why do I have to suffer also?

Christians must understand that Jesus Christ was hated by Satan and all the fallen angels, that He was hated by the Jewish leaders, and that He was hated by the philosophies of the world (self worship, idolatry, hedonism, and the worship of the creation). Therefore, *anyone* who openly identifies with Jesus Christ will be hated by all of His enemies. Christ warns his eleven disciples about what *they* can expect:

> *. . . They* (the Jewish leaders) *hated me without a cause* (John 15:25b). *They shall put you out of the synagogues; yea, the time cometh, that whosoever killeth you will think that he doeth God service* (John 16:2).
>
> *If ye were of the world, the world would love his own; but because ye are not of the world, but I have chosen you out of the world, therefore the world hateth you* (John 15:19). *. . . The servant is not greater than his lord. If they have persecuted me, they will also persecute you* (John 15:20b).

> *I pray not that thou shouldest take them out of the world, but that thou shouldest keep them from the evil* (John 17:15). (Part of Jesus' prayer on behalf of the eleven disciples.)

These eleven Apostles plus Paul were in high profile in the early church. Some evangelists and most pastors were also exposed to ready attack.

If you answer God's call for a leadership position in the church you should know what you are getting into and what it will take to succeed. *Always* remember, God does not leave you alone to suffer or be injured. The following verses will be invaluable to you as the battles rage:

> Romans 8:35 – *What shall separate us from the love of Christ? Shall tribulation, or distress, or persecution, or famine, or nakedness, or peril, or sword?* (See also II Timothy 2:3; Revelation 2:10.)
>
> James 5:10 – *Take, my brethren, the prophets who have spoken in the name of the Lord, for an example of suffering affliction, and of patience.* (See also I Peter 4:16, 19.)
>
> Philippians 4:13 – *I can do all things through Christ, who strengtheneth me.* (See also Matthew 28:20; Romans 8:31, 37; II Corinthians 2:14; Philippians 4:7, 19; Hebrews 13:5.)

The next chapter will describe some of the many blessings God has prepared for those who faithfully serve Him.

Isaiah 26:3 *Thou wilt keep him in perfect peace, whose mind is stayed on thee, because he trusteth in thee.*

Philippians 4:7 *And the peace of God, which passeth all understanding, shall keep your hearts and minds through Christ Jesus.*

Chapter 17

THE BENEFITS OF SUFFERING

The promises given above are to remind us that no matter how intense is the suffering that we might experience, *God has not lost control.* He not only carries us through the suffering, He gives us something unbelievable – peace and good cheer in tribulation (John 16:33), happiness if reproached for the name of Christ (I Peter 3:14), and happiness in endurance:

> James 5:11 – *Behold, we count them happy who endure. Ye have heard of the patience of Job, and have seen the end of the Lord, that the Lord is very pitiful, and of tender mercy.*

It has always seemed to me that God makes a quiet place in the midst of trouble for the believer's soul to rest and be revived. It is as if the believer who trusts in God is placed in the eye of a hurricane or tornado while the pressure churns around in the destructive whirlwind.

His body may be racked with pain, but his soul can be kept safe by the power of God. Maybe this is what Paul referred to in:

> II Corinthians 4:8, 9 – *We are troubled on every side, yet not distressed; we are perplexed, but not in despair; Persecuted, but not forsaken; cast down but not destroyed.*

The verse below indicates that the body can be virtually dying, but the soul will be protected – even renewed.

> II Corinthians 4:16 – *For which cause we faint not; but though our outward man perish, yet the inward man is renewed day by day.*

Verses 17 and 18 of II Corinthians places our physical suffering in an eternal perspective, i.e. "keep your eyes on God's eternal plan, not the physical universe which is soon to pass away."

> II Corinthians 4:17, 18 – *For our light affliction, which is but for a moment, worketh for us a far more exceeding and eternal weight of glory, While we look not at the things which are seen, but at the things which are not seen; for the things which are seen are temporal, but the things which are not seen are eternal.*

Blessings for a right attitude about current suffering could be received in time:

> Job 1:21b – *. . . The Lord gave, and the Lord hath taken away; blessed be the name of the Lord.* (Job's attitude.)

THE BENEFITS OF SUFFERING   177

Job 42:12a – *So the Lord blessed the latter end of Job more than his beginning;* (Job's blessings.)

Or, the blessing could be *no fear* at the point of death:

Psalm 23:4 – *Yea, though I walk through the valley of the shadow of death, I will fear no evil; for thou art with me; thy rod and thy staff they comfort me.*

Or, it could be the future joy God has prepared for those who have suffered:

Psalm 23:6 – *Surely goodness and mercy shall follow me all the days of my life; and I will dwell in the house of the Lord forever.* (See also John 14:2.)

II Corinthians 4:17 – *For our light affliction, which is but for a moment, worketh for us a far more exceeding and eternal weight of glory,*

Ephesians 2:7 – *That in the ages to come he might show the exceeding riches of his grace in his kindness toward us through Christ Jesus.*

II Timothy 2:12a – *If we suffer, we shall also reign with him;*

1 Peter 4:13 – *But rejoice, inasmuch as ye are partakers of Christ's sufferings, that, when his glory shall be revealed, ye may be glad also with exceeding joy.*

In any case our attitude toward suffering should always be *to count it all joy.*

Results of Suffering
(Spiritual Benefits and Blessings)

1. ***Warning of a broken fellowship with God.***
   Chastisement (the intentional infliction of pain for the purpose of correction) warns a believer to stop his rebellion (the knowing and willful breaking of God's standards) and to turn back to God (repent). (See Proverbs 3:11, 12; Hebrews 12:6; I John 1:9; Revelation 3:19.)

2. ***Teaching personal consequences for actions.***
   A penalty (the cost for breaking a law) is required to right a wrong. The penalty is the natural consequences for a specific wrongdoing. The guilty party is accountable to pay the penalty. (See Leviticus 24:17-22; Exodus 22:5, 6, 12, 14.)

3. ***Testing a believer's spiritual maturity.***
   Most tests, trials, or temptations take the form of suffering whereby man is challenged either to follow God's revealed Word (or to trust in His character); or instead to follow his sin nature or his own opinion. (See James 1:4; I Peter 1:6, 7.)

4. ***Learning obedience.***
   Obedience is foundational to the Christian Walk. When one suffers for righteousness or

THE BENEFITS OF SUFFERING 179

suffers without just cause, it develops obedience. (See Psalm 119:67; Philippians 2:8; Hebrews 5:8; I Peter 2:19-23.)

5. ***Developing Christian Character.***
Enduring suffering (particularly undeserved suffering) develops patience, perseverance, and hope (sure expectation). (See Romans 5:3, 4; James 1:3.)

6. ***Experiencing God's comfort.***
A believer who has received God's comfort during his suffering is equipped to comfort others who are suffering. (See II Corinthians 1:4-7; 7:6, 7; I Thessalonians 2:16, 17; 3:7.)

7. ***Bringing believers closer together.***
Fellowship (a sharing relationship based on common interest) within the body of Christ often comes about from the suffering of some. It should be exhibited in an all-for-one attitude (I Corinthians 12:26), by compassion (II Corinthians 7:7; Hebrews 10:34), by encouragement (I Thessalonians 4:18), by prayer (II Corinthians 1:11; Philippians 1:19), and by giving the necessities of life (Romans 15:26; II Corinthians 8:1-4; Philippians 4:14, 15; I Timothy 5:8; James 2:15; I John 3:17).

8. ***Bringing believers closer to God.***
Suffering has, as one of its natural byproducts the isolation of the sufferer from "normal" people. Isolation produces loneliness which can in turn produce depression. However, the closer such a one comes to know God and to have a personal relationship with Jesus Christ, the less isolated he will feel. Studying the

Word of God will allow a believer to hear God and praying will allow Him to hear the believer. (See Philippians 3:8-10.)

A PERSONAL TESTIMONY

"In the Introduction of this book I wrote about the loneliness that is a byproduct of suffering pain. Now, I would like to share with you some of the blessings that I have experienced because of that very same pain.

"Before illness interrupted my life, I was happiest when I was busy. I always found something to do and rarely had time just to sit down during the day. Even in the evenings I liked to keep my hands busy doing needlework. It was very frustrating when I began to experience various physical problems and eventually such pain that it was difficult to function as I once had done. I thought that a doctor, with all his modern equipment and lab tests, would be able provide a diagnosis and then prescribe a pill, a treatment, even a surgery that would eliminate that pain. At worse case, I envisioned being able to go home to be with the Lord where there would no longer be any pain or suffering. However, after spending thousands of dollars I was ill prepared to hear, 'There is nothing we can do. But it is not life threatening so learn to live with it the best you can.'

"Learn to 'live' with something that totally disrupts your life and turns every simple thing you try to do into a major chore? How could I? So, I tried all kinds of alternative ways to solve my problem – vitamins, herbs, acupuncture –nearly everything my well-meaning Christian friends recommended.

We spent thousands of dollars more on various 'miracle' cures, but I only grew worse over the years.

"Finally, I was confined to home most of the time, but I *was* 'learning to live with it,' although probably not in the way the doctors meant. The pain that wracked my body was driving me to pray frequently *(without ceasing* – I Thessalonians 5:17) to my Lord for comfort and guidance, and I was studying my Bible daily. Prayer and Bible study became my greatest joy and I increasingly thanked God for the time that I could rest in the encouragement that only God could provide (I Thessalonians 5:18). While enjoying my time with Him He was renewing my mind with His Word (II Corinthians 4:16) and I was filled with that peace that surpasses all understanding (Philippians 4:7). The pain even became my friend, reminding me when it was time to slow down and rest in the Lord. No greater happiness have I known in any activity than what I found during my quiet times alone with Him.

"God was training me during this time of prayer and Bible study. He lead me to understand human nature, especially my own (that was not fun, but necessary). He opened my eyes to sins in my life and things I needed to change and He taught me to forgive. He filled my heart with compassion for others' pain and my relationship with my husband became closer than ever before. And, He taught me many things that I needed to understand as preparation for events to come. Finally, I began to write, *On the Other Side of the Garden* – something I probably would have never 'gotten around to' if suffering had not become a part of my life.

"There were many trials and tests throughout the three years that it took to write my book. There were also many failures on my part. But God used all, even the failures to teach me more about Him and about His forgiveness. Nothing that happened, good or bad, was wasted if I but looked to Him for answers (Romans 8:28).

"I wish I could write about each thing that He did, but that is not possible at this time. However, I would like to share one additional blessing that I received about a year after I wrote my book. A pastor's wife asked me to speak at her women's retreat. We told her that I probably could not attend the retreat because I was in so much facial pain at the time that it was rendering me unable to speak more than a few words at a time. Nevertheless, she said that all the ladies agreed that they would 'pray me in.' My talk was to be, 'Praising God In All Things' and I prepared my speech. However, two weeks before the retreat it still looked impossible.

"Time was growing short and then just one week before the speech, two things happened. The first was the pain in my face improved and although it was still very painful for me to eat I could speak *pain free*. The second event was that Rick came home and informed me that he had just been terminated from his executive position – effective that very day.

"Praise God for His foreknowledge! *I thought I was studying in order to share with other women but that study was actually for me.* My immediate thought was, 'Thank you Lord for preparing me ahead of time for this trial.' It has been more than five years since that time and Rick and I have been through much trial and testing during the entire time. How grateful I am that my Lord taught me so much beforehand!

"What joy, what comfort, what peace has been provided to me by knowing my Savior, the Lord Jesus Christ. I have often wondered how anyone can endure the pressures of life without knowing Jesus. He deliberately came to earth as a man to suffer far more than any other human will ever suffer. Each of us are sinners and deserve death (Romans 5:12), yet He loved us so much that He bore our sins and died on the cross to provide salvation to anyone who will personally accept that He is the Son of God (John 3:16). And, just as He promised, He rose from the grave, went to heaven and is even now making a place for all those who believe (I Corinthians 15:3, 4; Matthew 14:2).

"Are you looking for love? You can receive no greater love than from the One who laid down His life for you. Are you looking for understanding? Who can understand more than He who suffered so greatly on your behalf? Are you fearful of death? Who can comfort more than He who is so powerful that He rose from the dead (Romans 14:9) and wants to prepare an eternal place for you in heaven? If you are a believer He has given you the Holy Spirit to encourage, assure, guide, and give you understanding of the Word of God. Are you looking for someone to talk to? Prayer is your answer.

"As I said, I often wonder how anyone can endure this life without knowing the Lord Jesus Christ. Who would want to turn their back on such a great salvation?"

Virginia Fugate

Now that you have read this very deep study on suffering, we recommend you immediately go back and read it again, or use it for a small study group. Its complexities will begin to disappear with familiarity. May God bless your study and your life's sufferings, whatever they may be.

J. Richard Fugate

APPENDICES

Appendix A

THE BIBLE AS A SOURCE OF INFORMATION FOR MAN

The following development sets forth why the author looks to the Bible for the truth man should live by, and this discussion establishes the Bible as the basic premise for this book.

God Exists

Genesis 1:1 – *In the beginning God created the heaven and the earth.*

Psalm 90:2 – *Before the mountains were brought forth, or ever thou hadst formed the earth and the world, even from everlasting to everlasting, thou art God.*

The Bible never attempts to prove or explain God's existence. It simply declares it to be true. This book, therefore, begins with this absolute: God's existence is certain truth. The Bible further states that no man can escape the recognition of the fact that God does exist:

> Romans 1:19, 20 – *Because that which may be known of God is manifest in them; for God hath shown it unto them. For the invisible things of him from the creation of the world are clearly seen, being understood by the things that are made, even his eternal power and Godhead, so that they are without excuse*;

Man may attempt to reject God, but man can never honestly deny his knowledge of God's existence. This passage reveals that God has made Himself known to man both rationally and empirically. The knowledge of the existence of God has been placed by God within the rational perception of man's mind. Creation, through its order and consistency, clearly presents the empirical proof of God the Creator. Acceptance of the knowledge of the existence of God as Creator will lead to the next logical assumption.

Mankind Exists as a Creation of God

> Genesis 1:27 – *So God created man in his own image, in the image of God created he him; male and female created he them.*

Man as a creature is dependent on his Creator, God. As Creator, God is responsible for His creation. To bring a creature into existence, but to fail to provide for the needs of that creature would be an act of irresponsibility. Because God cares for His creatures and takes full responsibility for His creation, He has provided for man's needs.

God Has Provided for Mankind's Physical Needs

> Genesis 1:28, 29 – *And God blessed them, and God said unto them, Be fruitful, and multiply, and fill the earth, and subdue it; and have dominion over the fish of the sea, and over the fowl of the air, and over every living thing that moveth upon the earth. And God said, Behold, I have given you every herb bearing seed, which is upon the face of all the earth, and every tree, in which is the fruit of a tree yielding seed; to you it shall be for food.*

The Hebrew word translated "to subdue" means "to tread down with the feet, to dominate;"[1] and the word translated "dominion" means "to rule."[2] Man was given the command to rule all earth's living creatures. He was given the command to control and use all earth's resources. God's provision for man's physical needs is the entire physical universe including air, water, land, plants, living creatures, and the climatic range required for man's existence. Physical science recognizes the extremely narrow range of environment in which man can survive and how perfectly it has been arranged to support all man's physical requirements.

Man is not merely a physical creation that exists in only a physical universe. He is also a creation of soul and spirit. As such, he has needs of the soul and the spirit, not just physical needs. In taking full responsibility for His creation, God has also provided for all man's soul and spiritual needs just as completely as He has for the physical.

God Has Provided for Mankind's Soul and Spiritual Needs

Matthew 4:4 – *But he answered and said, It is written, Man shall not live by bread alone, but by every word that proceedeth out of the mouth of God.*

Bread is the example of God's physical provision, while God's Word is God's provision for man's soul and spiritual life. God's Word has been provided for man's benefit. It has been recorded and preserved according to the faithfulness and justice of God. Because God cares for His creation, He has provided all that man needs to live; not only to survive physically, but to live abundantly in both soul and spirit.

Man was given the ability by God to subdue the physical universe and to rule the living things. Man was given strength and dexterity, but above all he was given mentality. With this mentality man could, on his own, discover the principles by which God governs the physical universe. Man has gradually obtained knowledge of the physical universe by observation of these natural laws, in other words, by science. Geology, astronomy, physiology, and mathematics are examples of true science. By contrast, the principles that govern the soul and spirit of man are not of a physical nature and cannot be discovered through the mentality of man.

Man has the need to understand his own soul, to know how to relate to other human beings, and to know his proper relationship with the physical universe. When man attempts to discover soul information by means of his own mentality apart from God's revelation, he is limited to his ability to observe and to reason. He therefore invents the pseudo-sciences of psychology, sociology, and anthropology in an attempt to answer man's soul questions and to solve man's soul problems.

Man also has the need to understand his spiritual relationship to His Creator, God. He needs to know where he came from, where he is going, who he is, and why he exists. Without knowing his own origin, destiny, make-up, and purpose, man is disoriented to life – even though he is physically alive. When man attempts to discover spiritual information by means of his own intellect apart from God's revelation, he develops various types of pseudo knowledge such as philosophy and religion, both of which are man-centered.

For soul and spiritual knowledge, man is totally dependent on God. Man cannot discover the principles that govern the soul or the spirit apart from the information that God has provided. God's Word is infinitely superior to any thought man could possibly have.

God's Thinking is Superior to Man's

> Isaiah 55:8, 9 – *For my thoughts are not your thoughts, neither are your ways my ways, saith the Lord. For as the heavens are higher than the earth, so are my ways higher than your ways, and my thoughts than your thoughts.*

God's thinking is far beyond the ability of man. It is foolish for man in his arrogance to question God's Word by means of his own viewpoint. As God declares:

> Proverbs 28:26a – *He that trusteth in his own heart is a fool,*

When God presents information on any subject, it will naturally conflict with the human systems of thinking. Human philosophy, psychology, sociology, or religion apart from God's Word is the attempt of mere man to organize thoughts that are inferior to God's thoughts. These systems of thinking must be evaluated by God's Word, not God's Word by them.

Each person's opinions are a combination of these human systems of thinking plus their own experiences. As the Biblical position is presented, it will be necessary for the reader to evaluate objectively his existing opinion by God's Word.

The Bible is God's Word

The Bible declares itself to be God's Word:

> 2 Timothy 3:16 – *All scripture is given by inspiration of God, and is profitable for doctrine, for reproof, for correction, for instruction in righteousness,*

> 2 Peter 1:20, 21 – *Knowing this first, that no prophecy of the scripture is of any private interpretation. For the prophecy came not at any time by the will of man, but holy men of God spoke as they were moved by the Holy Spirit.*

God did not cause His Word to be recorded for His own benefit, but to benefit mankind. It is a complete instruction manual containing soul and spiritual principles; therefore, mankind can look to the Bible for the information he needs on any moral or spiritual issue. The Bible has the answer for all of man's non-physical questions from eternal salvation to every practical matter in life. It is the only true source of moral and spiritual information by which man can successfully live each day. Since God's Word is to benefit man, it is meant to be understood.

Mankind is Meant to Understand God's Word

> Deuteronomy 29:29 – *The secret things belong unto the Lord our God; but those things which are revealed belong unto us and to our children forever, that we may do all the words of this law.*

God is infinite and omniscient. He has not revealed all His knowledge to finite man, but what He has revealed can both be understood and utilized. God's information is available to those who diligently search out its meaning and can be used successfully by those who accept its teaching. God has not hidden His soul and spiritual provision from mankind. God's Word is dependable and verifiably true.

God's Word Equals Truth

> John 17:17b – *Thy word is truth.*

It is impossible for God to lie (Hebrews 6:18). The Bible presents true principles (or laws) which can be applied in practice with predictable results. There are natural, fixed consequences for either observing or violating the soul and spiritual laws just as surely as for violating the physical laws. No man would expect to violate the law of gravity and not pay the consequences, but he will often foolishly violate soul and spiritual principles with total abandon. When physical laws are properly observed, the results are predictable and beneficial to man. Proper observance of the soul and spiritual principles will also produce consistent, beneficial results. God's Word declares the natural consequences of either observing or violating truth.

Observing Truth Results in Blessing
Violating Truth Results in Cursing

Deuteronomy 28:1, 2 – *And it shall come to pass, if thou shalt hearken diligently unto the voice of the Lord thy God, to observe and to do all his commandments which I command thee this day, that the Lord thy God will set thee on high above all nations of the earth; And all these blessings shall come on thee, and overtake thee, if thou shalt hearken unto the voice of the Lord thy God.*

Deuteronomy 28:15 – *But it shall come to pass, if thou wilt not hearken unto the voice of the Lord thy God, to observe to do all his commandments and his statutes which I command thee this day, that all these curses shall come upon thee, and overtake thee.*

Deuteronomy 30:19b – *I have set before you life and death, blessing and cursing; therefore, choose life, that both thou and thy seed may live,*

Joshua 1:8 – *This book of the law shall not depart out of thy mouth, but thou shalt meditate therein day and night, that thou mayest observe to do according to all that is written therein; for then thou shalt make thy way prosperous, and then thou shalt have good success.*

Footnotes

[1] Hebrew, *kabash* "subdue, bring into bondage, tread down with the feet;" thus "to dominate" (Zechariah 9:15; Micah 7:19; Jeremiah 34:11, 16; 2 Chronicles 28:10; Nehemiah 5:5). In Genesis 1:28 the aspect of "control" is evident and *kabash* is in the imperative mood of command. (Foundation for Biblical Research)

[2] Hebrew, *radah* "have dominion, rule, dominate" over someone or something; used here to indicate a position of dominance once the subduing has been accomplished. Like *kabash, radah* is a command. God commands man to "subdue" and then "rule" over that which has been subdued. (Ibid.)

Appendix B

ISRAEL AND THE LAW/ THE CHURCH AND THE NEW COVENANT

Israel's Promise Of Prosperity

God chose the nation of Israel as a peculiar[1] (precious possession) people above all other nations, *if* they would listen to Him and keep (obey) all His commandments:

> Deuteronomy 26:18 – *And the Lord hath avowed thee this day to be his peculiar people, as he hath promised thee, and that thou shouldest keep all his commandments.* (See also Exodus 19:5; Deuteronomy 7:6; 14:2; Psalm 135:4.)

Israel was to be so unique among the nations of the world that all peoples would be drawn to them to find *The God*. These other nations would be attracted to Israel because it would be so wise, powerful, rich, and prosperous.

> Deuteronomy 4:6b, 7 – *. . . for this is your wisdom and your understanding in the sight of the nations, who shall hear all these statutes and say, "Surely this great nation is a wise and understanding people. For what nation is there so great, who hath God as near unto them, as the Lord our God is in all things that we call upon him for?"*

> Isaiah 49:6b – *. . . I will also give thee for a light to the nations, that thou mayest be my salvation unto the end of the earth.* (See also Genesis 12:2,3; Exodus 19:6; Numbers 14:13-16; I Kings 4:29-34; 8:41-43; Jeremiah 33:9)

The Law

The Law is most often referred to as the Ten Commandments, the Law of Moses, or the Mosaic Law. Actually, it was the entire covenant God made with Israel as a nation. Theologians have divided it into three parts – commandments, judgments, and ordinances. Biblically they are referred to in total as The Commandments (order or decree), or as The Law (Romans 7:9-12). Together they make up a conditional covenant wherein God commits Himself to make Israel into a special nation above all other nations and to bless them if they will obey His covenant (the total law).

> Exodus 19:5 – *Now therefore, if ye will obey my voice indeed, and keep my covenant, then ye shall be a peculiar treasure unto me above all people; for all the earth is mine:*

The three divisions of the law are distinct in purpose:

1. **The Ten Commandments** establish moral absolutes for Israel (Exodus 20:1-17).

2. **The Judgments** are laws governing the peoples' interpersonal relationships like: personal injury issues, servant/master rights, private property rights, crimes against humanity (treatment of widows, the poor, orphans), usury, bribes, false testimony, etc. (Exodus 21:1 - 24:11).

3. **The Ordinances** governed the religious system – the tabernacle, the ark, the priesthood, the sacrifices, the Sabbath, etc. (Exodus 24:12 - 31:18).

God's Conditional Promises

Exodus 23:25 – *And ye shall serve the Lord your God, and he shall bless thy bread, and thy water; and I will take sickness away from the midst of thee.*

Chapter 28 of the book of Deuteronomy gives a list of specific blessings the nation of Israel would receive for obedience to God's laws:

Deuteronomy 28:2 – *And all these blessings shall come on thee, and overtake thee, if thou shalt hearken unto the voice of the Lord thy God.* (See also Joshua 1:7-8.)

Verses 3-14 enumerate many of Israel's blessings of prosperity in commerce, agriculture, propagation, farming, husbandry, warfare, and wealth. While there are no specific blessings of health in these passages, it will be clear in the next group that disobedience to God's laws would result in many types of illness.

> Deuteronomy 28:15 – *But it shall come to pass, if thou wilt not hearken unto the voice of the Lord thy God, to observe to do all his commandments and his statutes which I command thee this day, that all these curses shall come upon thee, and overtake thee.*

Verses 16-68 enumerate specific curses (consequences) Israel would face as a nation and as a people. Health wise this included deadly pestilence (verse 21); consumption, fever, and inflammation, extreme burning, blight, mildew (verse 22); tumors, scale, and itch without healing (verse 27); madness, blindness, and astonishment of heart (verse 28); plagues, and long-term severe sickness (verse 59), some leading to death.

The choice was up to the people. They knew the fantastic blessings of prosperity for obedience and they also knew the horrible consequences for disobedience. For the next 1400 years Israel vacillated between cursing and blessing.

What about today? Do the Ten Commandments have purpose for our nation? For Christians? Is it spiritual, moral, or even practical? The next section will answer these questions.

The Law and The Church

The Church (Christians since the time of Christ) has been concerned about what part The Law (specifically, the Ten Commandments) is supposed to have over The Church and its members. Let us look to God's Word to see if we can resolve this question, as well as what The Law has to do with suffering.

First of all, The Law was a covenant from God with Israel:

> Exodus 34:27 – *And the Lord said unto Moses, Write thou these words; for after the tenor of these words I have made a covenant with thee and with Israel.*
>
> Deuteronomy 4:13 – *And he declared unto you his covenant, which he commanded you to perform, even ten commandments; and he wrote them upon two tables of stone.*
>
> Deuteronomy 4:44 – *And this is the law which Moses set before the children of Israel:* (See also Leviticus 26:46; Deuteronomy 14:2.)

Second, this covenant was not intended for Gentile nations:

> Deuteronomy 4:8 – *And what nation is there so great, that hath statutes and ordinances as righteous as all this law, which I set before you this day?* (See also references to Israel as a peculiar people above all other nations.)

Third, the Old Testament (Covenant) Law was, in fact, specifically *not* given to the Church:

> Romans 6:14 – *For sin shall not have dominion over you; for ye are not under the law but under grace.*
>
> Galatians 2:16 – *Knowing that a man is not justified by the works of the law, but by the faith of Jesus Christ, even we have believed in Jesus Christ, that we might be justified by the faith of Christ, and not by the*

> works of the law; for by the works of the law shall no flesh be justified.

Galatians 5:18 – *But if ye be led by the Spirit, ye are not under the law.*

How the Law Relates to the Church

The Law as a covenant relationship with Israel was never meant to be entered into with The Church. This is not to say that portions of The Law do not have value for mankind today, but it is not the means for having a relationship with God. Nine of the Ten Commandments are restated in the New Testament as valid, moral laws for man to live by, and to protect a nation by means of severe consequences.

The Sabbath is the only commandment not so restated. If a Christian wishes to set aside Saturdays (the Sabbath) or any other day(s) of the week and dedicate that day(s) to worship, prayer, Bible study, and Christian fellowship, it would be a good practice. But, it is not a requirement of the New Covenant.

The second section of The Law, The Judgments, is the basis for most civil laws throughout the world. First and second degree murder are defined therein as well as manslaughter and the penalties for each. Personal damages and retribution for violated property rights are clearly spelled out along with honesty in testimony and exercising kindness toward others. Although these laws were meant for Hebrew to Hebrew and the nation of Israel, they still have value for civilized nations. However, while it is wrong to break many cf these standards, keeping these Judgments does not obtain or maintain a spiritual relationship with God for a Christian today.

The third section, The Ordinances (or the Priesthood), were specific to Israel's religious system. One who believes in "keeping The Commandments" today would need to keep all of these as well, just as the Jews incorrectly do in modern Israel. A short, enjoyable study will prove to the reader that Jesus Christ can be clearly seen in the symbols and the sacrifices of the Tabernacle. None of these Ordinances have any bearing on the Church. In fact, it is putting Christ to shame not to accept His new, high priesthood over the former Levitical priesthood:

> Hebrews 10:1 – *For the law, having a shadow of good things to come and not the very image of the things, can never with those sacrifices which they offered year by year continually make those who come to it perfect.*

> Hebrews 10:29 – *Of how much sorer punishment, suppose ye, shall he be thought worthy, who hath trodden under foot the Son of God, and hath counted the blood of the covenant, with which he was sanctified, an unholy thing, and hath done despite unto the Spirit of grace?*

Christ did not come to continue The Law but to complete its deficiencies.

> Matthew 5:17 – *Think not that I am come to destroy*[2] *the law, or the prophets; I am not come to destroy,*[2] *but to fulfill.*[3]

> Romans 10:4 – *For Christ is the end*[4] *of the law for righteousness to everyone that believeth.*

II Corinthians 3:11 – *For if that which is done away⁵ was glorious, much more that which remaineth is glorious."*

II Corinthians 3:13 – *And not as Moses, who put a veil over his face, that the children of Israel could not steadfastly look to the end⁴ of that which is abolished,⁵*

Ephesians 2:15a – *Having abolished⁵ in his flesh the enmity, even the law of commandments contained in ordinances, . . .*

Finally, what The Law could not do (provide a spiritual life) would be fulfilled by the Holy Spirit in the New Covenant:⁶

Romans 8:3, 4 – *For what the law could not do, in that it was weak through the flesh, God sending his own Son, in the likeness of sinful flesh and for sin, condemned sin in the flesh. That the righteousness of the law might be fulfilled in us, who walk not after the flesh, but after the Spirit.* (See also Jeremiah 31:31-34; Hebrews 8:7-15; 10:9.)

The Gentile nations would now be included in this New Covenant:

Ephesians 2:11-13 – *Wherefore, remember that ye, being in time past Gentiles in the flesh, who are called Uncircumcision by that which is called the Circumcision in the flesh made by hands – That at that time ye were without Christ, being aliens from the commonwealth of Israel, and strangers from the covenants of promise,*

> *having no hope, and without God in the world. But now in Christ Jesus ye who once were far off are made near by the blood of Christ.*

> Titus 2:14 – *Who gave himself for us that he might redeem us from all iniquity, and purify unto himself a people of his own, zealous of good works.*

> I Peter 2:9, 10 – *But ye are a chosen generation, a royal priesthood, an holy nation, a people of his own, that ye should show forth the praises of him who hath called you out of darkness into his marvelous light; Who in time past were not a people but are now the people of God; who had not obtained mercy but now have obtained mercy.*

The Church is now a new nation of priests to function through the High Priest, Jesus Christ, not through the Old Covenant. The Christian believer has been set free to observe God's commandments out of love, not bondage:

> I John 5:2, 3 – *By this we know that we love the children of God, when we love God, and keep his commandments. For this is the love of God, that we keep his commandments: and his commandments are not burdensome.*

In this we obey the essence of all The Law:

> Matthew 22:36-40 – *Master, which is the great commandment in the law? Jesus said unto him, Thou shalt love the Lord, thy*

God, with all thy heart, and with all thy soul, and with all thy mind. This is the first and great commandment. And the second is like it. Thou shalt love thy neighbor as thyself. On these two commandments hang all the law and the prophets.

Conclusion

A Jewish believer under the Old Testament had a great fringe benefit. He was guaranteed good health, financial prosperity, and safety in warfare, if he would keep all of The Law.

Even though the nation of Israel has been set aside, anyone who considers himself a Jew today is not cut off from the love of God. Under the Old Covenant, Gentiles had to become proselytes of Judaism and discover their relationship with God through the Ordinances (the sacrificial system). During The Church a Jew must find a personal relationship with God through Jesus Christ; i.e., become a Christian.

But, it is important to remember that Christians are not Jews, and The Church is not Israel. Keeping The Law is not the source of our blessings or cursings. God's plan for our spiritual nation is different from His plan for the physical nation of Israel (Romans 3:21-28). The next section will set forth The Church as the new chosen nation and explain why suffering is an integral part of our calling.

The New Covenant

The Church began with a bang on the day of Pentecost, exactly fifty days following the resurrection of the Lord Jesus Christ. The Holy Spirit made a dramatic display of sound and fire before indwelling approximately 120 disciples who had gathered at Mount Olivet (Olives) for this promised occurrence (Acts 1:4, 5, 15; 2:1-4). All of these disciples suddenly began to speak with languages other than their own native tongues, each of which was recognized by *"devout men, out of every nation under heaven"* who said, *"and how hear we every man **in our own tongue (language),** wherein we were born?"* (Acts 2:4-12).

This display was as dramatic as when God gave The Law to Israel (Exodus 19:18, 19; II Corinthians 3:7-11). The New Covenant was taking the place of the Old and the Mount of Olives was a fitting location. God later explained the Gentiles as being a wild olive branch grafted into the olive tree trunk that represented Israel (Romans 11:17).

Israel is not dead, but it is dormant *until the fullness of the Gentiles be come in* (Romans 11:24-27). However, The Law (Ten Commandments and Judgments) was abolished, done away with, brought to an end;" and the Ordinances were fulfilled by Jesus Christ once and for all when he died on the cross (II Corinthians 3:11, 13; Ephesians 2:15a). The moment that Jesus dismissed His spirit, the second veil in the Tabernacle was torn from top to bottom (Matthew 27:51) and He became the testator of the New Covenant (Hebrews 9:15-22). Under the Ordinances of the Law, this veil had separated all but the high priest from entering the presence of God (Hebrews 9:7-14). Now, every Christian in The Church is a priest and has access to the Father through Christ (I Peter 2:5; Ephesians 3:12; Hebrews 4:16). AMEN!

It should be obvious from the chart at the end of this chapter that Israel is the centerpiece of God's Plan for history. The fact that God set Israel aside for a short period and allowed the Gentiles to have their own spiritual nation is a blessing we should all appreciate. God's church is invisible and universal, but it is manifested by thousands of Bible-believing, local churches where Christ is proclaimed the Savior through His death, burial, and resurrection. It is only this Savior and only this message that *must be* truly accepted by an individual for his forgiveness of sin and his acceptance by God for eternal life.

> John 14:6 – *Jesus saith unto him, I am the way, the truth, and the life; no man cometh unto the Father, but by me.*

This act of accepting Christ on your part is a deep experience for your soul. It means seeing your sin as God sees you: *"But we are all as an unclean thing, and all our righteousnesses are as filthy rags;"* (literally: used menstrual rags – Isaiah 64:6). It also means humbling your pride enough to accept a grace gift far beyond your ability ever to repay. And, it means not *doing* anything yourself (such as law keeping) to earn even the wrapping on the gift.

> Titus 3:5a – *Not by works of righteousness which we have done, but according to his mercy he saved us,*

> II Corinthians 9:15 – *Thanks be unto God for his unspeakable gift.*

Only God is to be praised and glorified for the work of salvation.

Off with the Old, In with the New

God originally designed the New Covenant for Israel. (See Jeremiah 31:31-40.) The book of Joel reveals a little more about this event:

> Joel 2:28 – *And it shall come to pass afterward, that I will pour out my Spirit upon all flesh; and your sons and your daughters shall prophesy, your old men shall dream dreams, your young men shall see visions;*

Notice, God's Spirit (The Holy Spirit) is going to be given to *all* flesh (men, women, children). That indicates this future event is to occur at the beginning of the Millennium since this may be the only time in history that all flesh is saved. This is because the final judgment will have eliminated all unbelievers at the end of the tribulation. Also, the descriptions that follow in Joel 2:30-32; 3:1-17 appear to be that of the tribulation, and the Jeremiah passage suggests the rebuilding of Jerusalem (Jeremiah 31:38-40), which occurs during the Millennium.

When Israel rejected their Messiah, God set them aside and established The Church for both Jews and Gentiles. As previously described, the first Pentecost after Christ's death, burial, and resurrection, the Holy Spirit was poured out on everyone who had been called to gather on Mt. Olivet (Acts 2:1-4; 2:16,17). Anyone who knew the Scriptures would have recognized this event as being very similar to the Joel 2 and 3 discourse, *but that at this time it was not directed to the house of Israel or the house of Judah.* It would have been immediately clear that Israel had been set aside and that The Church was now receiving blessings from God.

Of course the New Covenant is mentioned in relationship to the communion table (Luke 22:20 and I Corinthians 11:25); but the real proof that the Church is under the New Covenant, which will be given to Israel at a later date, is:

> II Corinthians 3:6 – *Who also hath made us able ministers[7] of the new testament, not of the letter, but of the spirit; for the letter killeth, but the Spirit giveth life.*

Here, Paul states that God made them (the Apostles of The Church) competent (or qualified) servers of a New Covenant. He then made it clear he was speaking of the spiritual covenant, *not* the written one. (See verses 7-9.)

Summary

At this point we should all be in agreement:

- As born-again Christians we are born from above and therefore spiritually alive, our soul is saved from future judgment, and we are guaranteed a super-special body in eternity.

- We are not part of the nation of Israel or under the old covenant.

- We are members of The Church and desire to know and to live God's will for our lives.

The chart on the following page should help to visualize the times of the Jews and the time of the Gentiles.

APPENDIX B

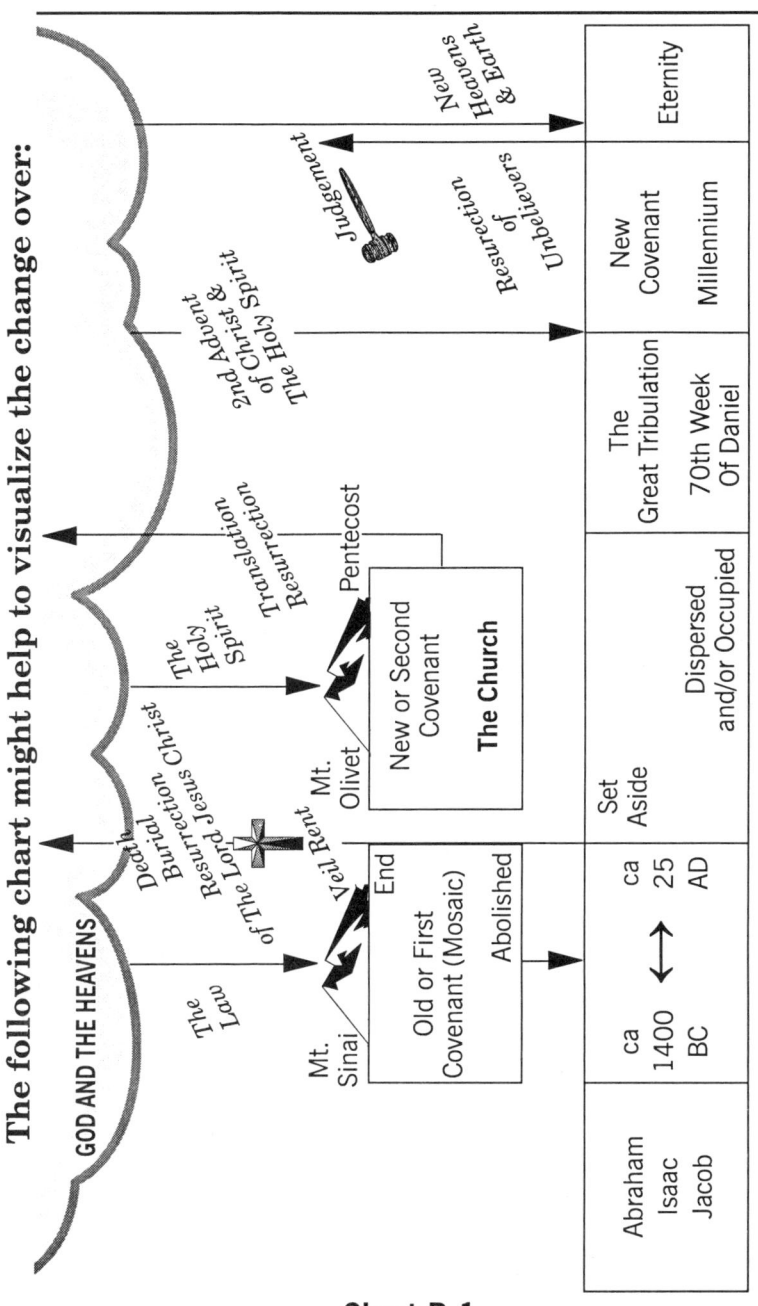

Chart B.1

[1] Hebrew, *Segullah*, a precious treasure, or valuable possession.

[2] Greek, *kataluo*, "to demolish" met. "to nullify." Foundation for Biblical Research ™

[3] Greek, *pleroo*, "this word has several aspects to its meaning – to fill up, to satisfy a deficiency by filling, to influence (to pervade). Here the idea is *to complete its deficiency* of not being able to impart spiritual life" (Romans 8:3) (Ibid.)

[4] Greek, *telos* , "attainment of the end purpose, absolute end." (Ibid.)

[5] Greek, *katargew*, "here the present, passive, participle translated being done away, lit. not working, or completely ineffective." (Ibid.)

[6] The New Covenant: Luke 22:20; I Corinthians 11:25; II Corinthians 3:6; Hebrews 8:8-13 cp Jeremiah 31:31-34; Hebrews 9:15; 12:24.

[7] Greek, *Doulos*, "One who is a servant or attendant."

APPENDIX C

GREEK WORDS RELATING TO SUFFERING

A summary of the approach utilized by Foundation for Biblical Research™ (FBR) in determining Biblical word meanings is all that will be covered in this appendix. Not all of the steps are shown.

First, a list of words from the English Bible (King James Version, Scofield Edition) were selected that fell within the semantic domain of the subject area pertaining to SUFFERING.

Second, a cross list of Greek and Hebrew words for the English words in step one was made. (Only the Greek development is contained herein.)

Third, a word study was performed on each individual word and its use in all contexts. Every occurrence of the word was checked. It's morphology, syntax, use of the article, and comparison/contrasts with other words were noted.

Fourth, a hypothesis was drawn based upon the data.

Fifth, unresolved problems were noted for future analysis.

Sixth, a specific analysis was made where more than one of the words within the semantic domain occurred together in the same context.

Seventh, the resultant data was compared to the hypothesis which was altered accordingly (when needed).

Eighth, lexicons were studied for each word's etymology and extra-Biblical usage. The results of this step were compared to the hypothesis mentioned in step four. This was done to evaluate lexical data by Biblical data. (The lexical data was dealt with subsequent to the Biblical data to ensure that the veil of previous human studies did not cloud what the Bible had to say about the use of the word.)

Ninth, the hypothetical meaning (or derived Biblical meaning) was checked against lexical data and deviations were evaluated and noted.

Tenth, a conclusion was then arrived at with regard to specific Biblical meanings of each word.

Eleventh, a chart was then drawn to denote the relationships between the words in the semantic domain of suffering.

This procedure was devised in order to assist the serious student in better understanding what God's Word precisely communicates.

English Words

In researching the English language for words that described suffering, we identified over one hundred seventy words within that semantic domain. Several groupings could be made to help categorize these words:

- **Tribulation** – Natural catastrophe or disaster, usually on a national or worldwide basis. Earthquake, flood, hurricane, tornado, fire, hail, meteors, drought, famine, plaque, pestilence, and war.

- **Death** – Natural, unnatural, murder, suicide, manslaughter, deadly accident, execution.

- **Physical Attack** – Assault, strike, fight, revolt, persecute, abuse, rape, torture, molest, ill-treat, stings, bites, boils, sores, cancer, rupture, broken bone, sprain, surgery, cut, bruise, wound.

- **Personal Tragedy** – Hurtful accident (mutilate, mar, disfigure, amputate, deform), affliction, trial, trouble, ordeal, injustice, evil, illegal, immoral, injury, harm, physical or mental illness, sickness, hurt, hardship, pressure, decline, adversity, addiction, poverty, destitute, fired, abandonment, separation, divorce, rejected, expelled, bankrupt (failure, ruin, guilt, transgression, sinfulness, crime, delinquent, defraud, insolvent), privation (meager), exploited, spurned, misunderstood, cursed, denounced, ridiculed, unappreciated, disabled, false accusation, lies, gossip and addiction.

- **Emotional Pain** – Anguish, anxiety, grief, misery, sorrow, bitterness, despair, heartache, ail, agony, irritation, loneliness, isolation, regret, homesick, estranged, sad, weep, cry, regret, irritation, bored, frustration, disappointment, humiliation, depression, worthlessness, embarrassed, jealousy, hatred, envy, fear.

Words In The Semantic Range Of
"SUFFERING"

GREEK TRANSLITERATION	ENGLISH TRANSLATION (KJV)
adikeo	to be unjust, wrong
agonizomai	to contend, struggle, fight
agrupneo	to watch without sleep, vigilant
anagkazo	to be compelled, obligated – necessity
anechomai	to suffer, bear, endure
apokeino	to kill, destroy
astheneo	to be sick, weak, infirm
atheteo	to reject, despise (frustrate?)
barus	grievous
dero	to beat, smite, skin, scourge,
desmeo	to bind (like prisoner)
dioko	to persecute, to follow after, hound
dokimazo	to approve by test, acceptable, proven, assay metal for precious
enochos (N)	guilty of, subject to
hubris	hurt, injury
hupomeno	to endure, take patiently, abide
hustereo	to fall behind, lack, fail
kakopoieo	to do evil
kakos	bad, evil, harm, hurt
klaio	to weep, cry
kolaphizo	to beat with fist
loidoreo	to revile
lupeo	to distress, pain, grief, sorrow
nesteuo	to fast, want of food

oneidizo	to revile, reproach, upbraid
pascho	to suffer, affliction, passion, death
peirazo	to tempt, a temptation, trail, prove
pentheo	to morn, grieve
phobeo	to fear
pikraino	be bitter, make bitter
plesso	to strike a blow, plague, afflict
ptocheia	to be poor, to beg
pturo	to terrify
pulemeo	to fight or quarrel, strife
purosis	burning trial
skolops (N)	thorn, pointed, plague
stenazo	groan
stenochoreo	to cramp, restrict, distress
strateia (N)	Warfare
sumpascho	to hold together, constrain, compress
sunecho	to hold together, constrain, compress
suro	to draw, drag (out of house)
suntribo	to break in pieces, bruise
talairoria	distress, misery, wretched
tarrasso	to agitate water, to stir up
tapeinos	humble, make low
thlibo	to afflict, trouble, burden, persecute, throng, narrow (stress?)
tlege	to strike someone

These forty-eight Greek words are used to express pain and suffering in the New Testament. The Biblical meaning of each word will have to wait for the second edition of this book.

Bibliography

Scofield, C.I., ed. *Holy Bible* (Authorized King James Version). New York: Oxford University Press, 1967.

The Compact Edition of the Oxford English Dictionary, 1971.

* The Foundation for Biblical Research ™ utilized the following resource books in their research. (This is only a selected list.)

Abbott-Smith, G. A. *A Manual Greek Lexicon of the New Testament.* Edinburgh: T. & T. Clark, 1937.

Alsop, John R. *Index to the Bauer-Arndt-Gingrich Greek Lexicon.* Grand Rapids: Zondervan Publishing House, 1968.

Arndt, William F. and Gingrich, F. Wilbur. *A Greek-English Lexicon of the New Testament.* Chicago: University of Chicago Press, 1957.

Botterweck, G., and Ringgren, H., ed. *Theological Dictionary of the Old Testament.* Grand Rapids: Wm. B. Eerdmans Publishing Co. Vol. I & II (revised edition) 1977; Vol. III, 1978.

Brown, Francis; Driver, S.R.; and Briggs, Charles A., eds. *A Hebrew and English Lexicon of the Old Testament,* 1929. Reprint. Oxford: At the Clarendon Press, 1974.

The New Testament (Textus Receptus). London: Trinitarian Bible Society, 1977.

Einspahr, Bruce. *Index to Brown, Driver & Briggs.* Chicago: Moody Press, 1976.

Gesenius, William. *Hebrew-Chaldee Lexicon to the Old Testament.* Trans. Samuel P. Tregelles. Grand Rapids: Wm. B. Eerdmans Publishing Co., 1949.

Girdlestone, Robert B. *Synonyms of the Old Testament.* 2nd ed. 1897. Reprint. Grand Rapids: Wm. B. Eerdmans Publishing Co, 1956.

Kittel, R. *Biblia Hebraica*, 3rd Ed. Stuttgart: Wurtetembergische Bibelanstalt, 1961.

Kittel, R. *Theological Dictionary of the New Testament.* 10 vols. Grand Rapids: Wm. B. Eerdmans Publishing Co., 1964

Liddell, Henry George and Scott, Robert. *A Greek-English Lexicon.* Oxford: Oxford University Press, 1940.

Moulton, James Hope and Milligan, George. *The Vocabulary of the Greek Testament.* Grand Rapids: Wm. B. Eerdmans Publishing Co., 1952.

Thayer, Joseph Henry. *Greek-English Lexicon of the New Testament*. Grand Rapids: Zondervan Publishing House, 1976.

The Greek New Testament, 3rd ed. London: The United Bible Societies, 1975.

Trench, Richard C. *Synonyms of the New Testament*. Grand Rapids: Wm. B. Eerdmans Publishing Co., 1880.

Edman, V. Raymond. *They Found the Secret*. Grand Rapids: Zondervan Publishing House, 1984

Compiled and Edited by, Robert K. Brown and Mark R. Norton. Devotions written by, William J. Petersen and Randy Petersen. *The One Year Book of Hymns*. Wheaton: Tyndale House Publishers, Inc., 1995.

In Touch Ministries. Web site: www.intouch.org, 1999

The Bible Companion Series. Integrated Systems Solutions Corporation (A Wholly-Owned IBM Subsidiary) IBM. White Harvest Software, Inc., 1995

Gramcord for Windows. The Gramcord Institute. Web site: www.GRAMCORD.org, 1999

If your local Christian Bookstore does not stock all of the Foundation for Biblical Research™ titles, you may order directly:

Christian Books and Gifts On-Line
www.rfugate.com   E-mail: cbg@rfugate.com
Phone/Fax 602/431-8975
J. Richard & Virginia Fugate
2401 W. Southern Ave. #219
Tempe, AZ 85282

You may place your order by phone, e-mail, this order form, or you may print and mail our more complete form available at our website. Please send check with order.

Item		Price	Total
What The Bible Says About™ Suffering	____	$12	$_____
What The Bible Says About™ Child Training 2nd	____	$13	$_____
What The Bible Says About™ Child Training 2nd Video Set	____	$150	$_____
What The Bible Says About™ Child Training 2nd Audio Set	____	$42	$_____
On The Other Side Of The Garden	____	$9	$_____
On The Other Side Of The Garden Workbook	____	$13	$_____
No Place Like Home School	____	$7	$_____

Subtotal _____
15% Discount off Subtotal − _____
10% Shipping & Handling ($3.00 Min.) + _____
ORDER TOTAL $ _____

Name _____
Mailing Address _____
City, State, Zip _____
Phone (____) _____
If Pastor, Name of Church _____